Montgomery County-Norristown
Public Library

**This project is made possible
through a grant from the Institute of Museum
and Library Services as administered by
Pennsylvania Department of Education
and the Commonwealth of Pennsylvania,
Tom Corbett, Governor**

UNDERSTANDING DRUGS

Cancer Treatment Drugs

TITLES IN THE *UNDERSTANDING DRUGS* SERIES

UNDERSTANDING DRUGS

Cancer Treatment Drugs

ALAN HECHT

CONSULTING EDITOR
DAVID J. TRIGGLE, Ph.D.
University Professor
School of Pharmacy and Pharmaceutical Sciences
State University of New York at Buffalo

CHELSEA HOUSE
P U B L I S H E R S
An imprint of Infobase Publishing

Chelsea House
An imprint of Infobase Publishing
132 West 31st Street
New York NY 10001

Library of Congress Cataloging-in-Publication Data

Hecht, Alan.
  Cancer treatment drugs / Alan Hecht.
    p. cm. — (Understanding drugs)
  Includes bibliographical references and index.
  ISBN-13: 978-1-60413-535-0 (hardcover : alk. paper)
  ISBN-10: 1-60413-535-2 (hardcover : alk. paper)   1. Antineoplastic agents—Popular works.   I. Title.   II. Series.
  RC271.C5H43 2010
  616.99'4061—dc22   2010026380

Chelsea House books are available at special discounts when purchased in bulk quantities for businesses, associations, institutions, or sales promotions. Please call our Special Sales Department in New York at (212) 967-8800 or (800) 322-8755.

You can find Chelsea House on the World Wide Web at
http://www.chelseahouse.com

Text design by Kerry Casey
Cover design by Alicia Post
Composition by Newgen North America
Cover printed by Bang Printing, Brainerd, MN
Book printed and bound by Bang Printing, Brainerd, MN
Date printed: December 2010
Printed in the United States of America

10 9 8 7 6 5 4 3 2 1

This book is printed on acid-free paper.

All links and Web addresses were checked and verified to be correct at the time of publication. Because of the dynamic nature of the Web, some addresses and links may have changed since publication and may no longer be valid.

Contents

foreword

THE USE AND ABUSE OF DRUGS

For thousands of years, humans have used a variety of sources with which to cure their ills, cast out devils, promote their well-being, relieve their misery, and control their fertility. Until the beginning of the twentieth century, the agents used were all of natural origin, including many derived from plants as well as elements such as antimony, sulfur, mercury, and arsenic. The sixteenth-century alchemist and physician Paracelsus used mercury and arsenic in his treatment of syphilis, worms, and other diseases that were common at that time; his cure rates, however, remain unknown. Many drugs used today have their origins in natural products. Antimony derivatives, for example, are used in the treatment of the nasty tropical disease leishmaniasis. These plant-derived products represent molecules that have been "forged in the crucible of evolution" and continue to supply the scientist with molecular scaffolds for new drug development.

Our story of modern drug discovery may be considered to start with the German physician and scientist Paul Ehrlich, often called the father of chemotherapy. Born in 1854, Ehrlich became interested in the ways in which synthetic dyes, then becoming a major product of the German fine chemical industry, could selectively stain certain tissues and components of cells. He reasoned that such dyes might form the basis for drugs that could interact selectively with diseased or foreign cells and organisms. One of Ehrlich's early successes was development of the arsenical "606"—patented under the name *Salvarsan*—as a treatment for syphilis. Ehrlich's goal was to create a "magic bullet," a drug that would target only the diseased cell or the invading disease-causing organism and have no effect on healthy cells and tissues. In this he was not successful, but his great research did lay the groundwork for the successes of the twentieth century, including the discovery of the sulfonamides and the antibiotic penicillin. The latter agent saved countless lives

6

during World War II. Ehrlich, like many scientists, was an optimist. On the eve of World War I, he wrote, "Now that the liability to, and danger of, disease are to a large extent circumscribed—the efforts of chemotherapeutics are directed as far as possible to fill up the gaps left in this ring." As we shall see in the pages of this volume, it is neither the first nor the last time that science has proclaimed its victory over nature, only to have to see this optimism dashed in the light of some freshly emerging infection.

From these advances, however, has come the vast array of drugs that are available to the modern physician. We are increasingly close to Ehrlich's magic bullet: Drugs can now target very specific molecular defects in a number of cancers, and doctors today have the ability to investigate the human genome to more effectively match the drug and the patient. In the next one to two decades, it is almost certain that the cost of "reading" an individual genome will be sufficiently cheap that, at least in the developed world, such personalized medicines will become the norm. The development of such drugs, however, is extremely costly and raises significant social issues, including equity in the delivery of medical treatment.

The twenty-first century will continue to produce major advances in medicines and medicine delivery. Nature is, however, a resilient foe. Diseases and organisms develop resistance to existing drugs, and new drugs must constantly be developed. (This is particularly true for anti-infective and anticancer agents.) Additionally, new and more lethal forms of existing infectious diseases can develop rapidly. With the ease of global travel, these can spread from Timbuktu to Toledo in less than 24 hours and become pandemics. Hence the current concerns with avian flu. Also, diseases that have previously been dormant or geographically circumscribed may suddenly break out worldwide. (Imagine, for example, a worldwide pandemic of Ebola disease, with public health agencies totally overwhelmed.) Finally, there are serious concerns regarding the possibility of man-made epidemics occurring through the deliberate or accidental spread of disease agents—including manufactured agents, such as smallpox with enhanced lethality. It is therefore imperative that the search for new medicines continue.

All of us at some time in our life will take a medicine, even if it is only aspirin for a headache or to reduce cosmetic defects. For some individuals, drug use will be constant throughout life. As we age, we will likely be exposed to a variety of medications—from childhood vaccines to drugs to relieve pain caused by a terminal disease. It is not easy to get accurate and understandable information about the drugs that we consume to treat diseases and disorders. There are, of course, highly specialized volumes aimed at medical or scientific professionals. These, however, demand a sophisticated knowledge base and experience to be comprehended. Advertising on television is widely available but provides only fleeting information, usually about only a single drug and designed to market rather than inform. The intent of this series of books, **Understanding Drugs**, is to provide the lay reader with intelligent, readable, and accurate descriptions of drugs, why and how they are used, their limitations, their side effects, and their future. The series will discuss both *"treatment drugs"*—typically, but not exclusively, prescription drugs, that have well-established criteria of both efficacy and safety—and *"drugs of abuse,"* agents that have pronounced pharmacological and physiological effects but that are, for a variety of reasons, not to be considered for therapeutic purposes. It is our hope that these books will provide readers with sufficient information to satisfy their immediate needs and to serve as an adequate base for further investigation and for asking intelligent questions of health care providers.

—David J. Triggle, Ph.D.
University Professor
School of Pharmacy and Pharmaceutical Sciences
State University of New York at Buffalo

1
Cancer: What Is It and How Does It Affect the Body?

Joe had been a heavy smoker for 30 years. Finishing one to two packs of cigarettes each day was commonplace. He never thought anything of it and ignored the various warnings from the U.S. Surgeon General that were printed on each pack he smoked. When he developed a cough that lasted for several months, some mild chest pain, a loss of appetite, and weight loss, he attributed it to chronic bronchitis that caused him to feel out of sorts and went to his family doctor to get some antibiotics that he was sure would clear up the cough.

His doctor, upon examining him and taking a history of the condition, immediately sent Joe to the radiologist for a chest X-ray. The radiologist's report was far from encouraging. The films showed a mass with ill-defined borders in his right lung. This was suggestive of small-cell lung cancer. Joe was sent to an oncologist (a cancer specialist) to determine how serious his cancer was and what procedures should be used to treat it.

After several other tests, including a biopsy and MRI, the oncologist decided that this type of cancer would respond best to chemotherapy—the use of anticancer drugs to help shrink the tumor and slow down or stop the progression of the cancer so that more tissues might not become affected by cancerous cells that could migrate out of the lung (a process known as metastasis). Joe began treatment within a few days.

WHAT ARE ANTICANCER DRUGS?

Cancer has been a scourge of the human race since it developed tens of thousands of years ago. The death rate in the United States alone exceeded 565,000 in 2008. The number of people who developed new cancer cases was approximately 1.5 million. Worldwide, it is estimated that there were some 10.9 million new cancer diagnoses and almost 7 million deaths. Clearly, this is a disease that requires treatment in many forms, one of which is chemotherapy.[1]

There are many types of cancer, and each individual reacts to medications in his or her own way. Because their response to medications may vary, the need arose for the development of different kinds of medications that would attack cancerous cells in different ways. Some, like daunomycin cerubidine, are cytolytic. That is, they cause the cells to break open. Others, like cytarabine, affect DNA synthesis. There are many other drugs with several other modes of action, and new medications are still being created that will, it is hoped, work better than those now available.

Using chemicals to treat cancer dates back to the early twentieth century when mustard gas, originally used during World War I as a chemical warfare agent, was shown to lower the white blood cell count of those exposed to it. Two pharmacologists, Louis Goodman and Alfred Gilman, theorized that if the mustard gas caused a reduction in the white blood cell count, it might have the same effect on cancer cells.[2]

A patient with non-Hodgkin's **lymphoma**, a solid tumor in the lymphatic system, was given mustine, a compound related to mustard gas, intravenously rather than having to breathe in the irritating gas as the World War I soldiers did. He showed a marked, but temporary, improvement in his condition. A more detailed review of the history of anticancer drugs and how they work will be presented later in this book.[3]

WHAT IS CANCER?

Cancer: The word strikes fear into the hearts of most people who hear it. The word originally came from the Greeks when Hippocrates (460 BC-370 BC), a Greek physician, observed cancerous tumors and noted that their appearance was similar to that of a crab with swollen veins. He used the words "carcinoma" and "carcinos" to describe the tumors and called cancer "karkinos"

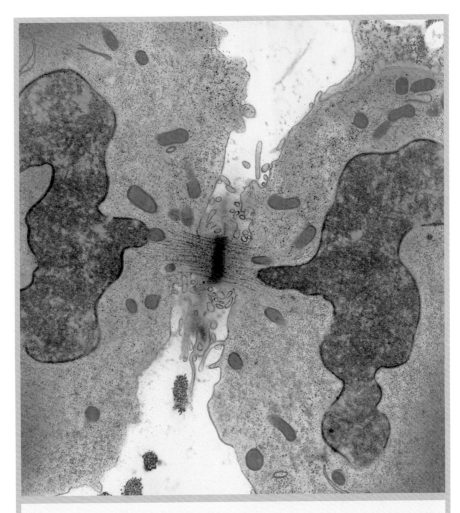

Figure 1.1 Dividing cancer cell. Colored transmission electron (TEM) of a section through a cancer cell undergoing mitotic cell division. The cell is in telophase, the last stage of mitosis. Nuclear envelopes have formed around the duplicate chromosome sets creating two nuclei (green). The cytoplasm (orange) contains mitochondria (red). The two daughter cells are connected by a narrow cytoplasmic bridge (at center). *(©Quest/Photo Researchers, Inc.)*

which means crab. The first documented description of cancer came out of Egypt around 1500 B.C. when physicians described eight cases of breast tumors and recorded them on papyrus. They described the treatment with cauterization (destruction by heat) and the fact that there was no cure, only palliative measures to make the patient feel more comfortable.

There are many different types of cancer that affect numerous organs and areas of the body. Generally speaking, it is a disease associated with rapid growth of the affected cells, often developing into a tumor. These cells have a propensity for invading surrounding tissues and even tissues at sites distant from the original cancer (**metastasis**). The causes of cancer are many and include genetics, environmental factors such as chemical toxins, radiation sources, ultraviolet rays from the sun and other sources, viruses, and various other factors.

All forms of cancer share two things in common: uncontrolled growth and invasion of surrounding tissues. At times, cancer may spread to distant sites, as noted above. Cancer cells ignore the built-in controls that govern normal cells. One of these is contact inhibition. This regulatory mechanism causes normal cells to recognize the fact that they are in contact with a neighboring cell and must stop growing. It's something like respecting the fence between your property and your neighbor's.

Almost all cancers are associated with genetic abnormalities in the cancer cells themselves. The causes of these abnormalities vary and may include exposure to **carcinogens** (substances known to be associated with a high incidence of cancer) such as cigarette smoke, exposure to large doses of ultraviolet radiation, and certain viruses. Some genetic abnormalities run in families and may be inherited. Others occur spontaneously for reasons that are not yet understood. In the end, the cancer cells exhibit several structural differences when compared to normal cells.[4]

It has been found that specific types of genes, known as **oncogenes**, are activated in cancerous cells. These cancer-promoting genes are "turned off" in normal cells. Their activation allows cancer cells to undergo hyperactive growth and abnormal cell division as well as protecting them against **apoptosis**, the genetically programmed cell death that occurs in all normal cells at a predetermined time in their life cycle. The cancer cells become a sort of "super cell," successfully ignoring the "rules" that other cells must follow.

Another set of genes known as **tumor suppressor genes** becomes inactivated, thus allowing the growth and development of tumors. Now the cancer cells are able to reprogram their normal cell cycle, escape capture by the immune system, and replicate their DNA in an abnormal way that helps to create the devastating conditions associated with cancers.

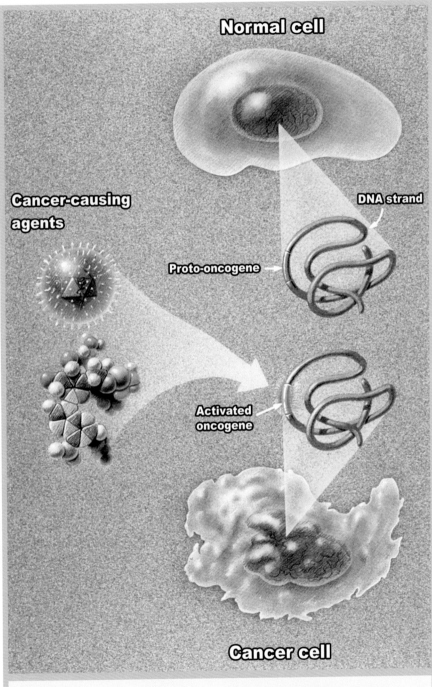

Figure 1.2 Illustration shows activation of oncogene by cancer-causing agent, leading to creation of cancer cell. *(National Cancer Institute)*

THE PREVALENCE OF CANCER

Many factors help to determine the prevalence of the different forms of cancer in a particular population. For the most part, it is hard to predict who will develop cancer and who will not. Several people may be exposed to the same probable cause, but only some of them will develop a particular type of cancer. Why this occurs is still not well understood.

Although there are many probable causes of the different forms of cancer, several are considered to be the most common risk factors.[5]

AGING

As the body ages, the incidence of cancers increases. A valid explanation of this focuses on the increasing number of **senescent** cells that develop with age. Research using yeast cells has shown that as these cells age, they develop genetic instability, which is a common finding in cancer cells. The research showed that as the yeast cells reached late middle age, the incidence of mutated chromosomes increased by 200 times. This discovery helps to explain the prevalence of cancer among seniors. According to the American Cancer Society, almost 80% of cancers are diagnosed after age 55.[6]

TOBACCO USE

Smoking has been linked to at least 15 different types of cancer and is known to damage virtually every organ in the body. Tobacco is considered to be one of the strongest cancer-causing agents among humans. It has been linked to several different forms of cancer, most commonly lung cancer. It has also been associated with chronic lung disease and cardiovascular diseases.[7]

Cigarette smoking is the major preventable cause of death in the United States, leading to an estimated 438,000 deaths per year. In addition, exposure to secondhand smoke is estimated to cause approximately 38,000 deaths per year. Secondhand smoke is the smoke that leaves the tip of the cigarette and escapes into the air that other people are breathing. In essence, these people are actually smoking (without the presumed benefit of any filtration) a percentage of the cigarette that the smoker is smoking.[8]

Smoking also increases the risk of many other types of cancer, including cancers of the throat, mouth, pancreas, kidney, bladder, and cervix.

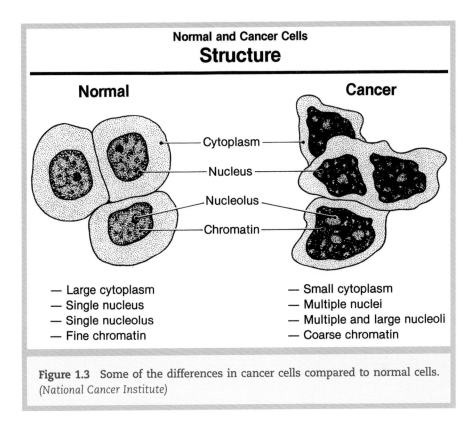

Figure 1.3 Some of the differences in cancer cells compared to normal cells. (*National Cancer Institute*)

Furthermore, smokers are up to 6 times more likely to have a heart attack. This risk increases in direct proportion to the number of cigarettes smoked. In 2007 approximately 19.7% of adults were smokers, according to the Centers for Disease Control and Prevention. Today, 23% of high school students and 8% of middle school students are smokers.

SUNLIGHT

Sunlight contains three types of radiation. The first is visible light. Obviously, this is what we are able to see. Visible light contains the colors that mix together to make white light. The second is infrared radiation, which provides the warmth we feel. The third is ultraviolet (UV) radiation.

UV radiation is the only portion of sunlight that has been linked to causing cancers. It exists in three forms. The first is ultraviolet A, which is long-wave ultraviolet radiation. The second is ultraviolet B, which causes sunburns. The

Table 1.1 Types of Ultraviolet Radiation and Their Features	
Ultraviolet Radiation Type	General Features
Ultraviolet A radiation (UVA, long-wave UV)	Not filtered out in the atmosphere Passes through glass Produces some tanning Once considered harmless but now believed harmful Levels remain relatively constant throughout the day
Ultraviolet B radiation (UVB, sunburn radiation)	Some filtered out in the atmosphere by the ozone layer Does not pass through glass Causes sunburn, tanning, wrinkling, aging of the skin, and skin cancer Highest intensity at noontime
Ultraviolet C radiation (UVC, short-wave UV)	Filtered out in the atmosphere by the ozone layer before reaching Earth Major artificial sources are germicidal lamps Burns the skin and causes skin cancer
Source: Canadian Centre for Occupational Health and Safety. "Skin Cancer and Sunlight." URL: http://www.ccohs.ca/oshanswers/diseases/skin_cancer.html. Accessed on September 25, 2009.	

third is ultraviolet C, which is short-wave radiation. Table 1.1 summarizes the different types of UV radiation and their characteristics.

Sunlight affects the skin in several ways. The most common is a sunburn. Basically, this is an inflammatory reaction to the damage caused by exposure to excessive sunlight. It can be painful and cause peeling of the skin. Studies have shown that brief, severe sunburns in childhood as well as long-term exposure to sunlight may cause several different forms of skin cancer years later. These include basal cell carcinoma and cutaneous malignant melanoma. Chronic exposure is linked to the development of squamous cell carcinoma.[9]

When skin cells are exposed to UV radiation, changes in their DNA may take place that affect the skin's appearance and normal cellular growth. In addition to a sunburn and possible cancer, the skin tends to age more rapidly and become more wrinkled.

IONIZING RADIATION

Ionizing radiation is associated with X-rays, the Sun, radioactive substances that exist in nature and those that are used for diagnosis and treatment of several diseases. The high energy contained in these sources causes the loss of electrons from atoms or molecules in cells, thus creating **ions**. Ions are also referred to as free radicals. The free radicals are searching for electrons to pair with because nature "dislikes" unpaired electrons. These free radicals will interact with proteins, enzymes, and structures within the cell, leading to cellular damage and, in many cases, cancer.

GENETICS

Several cancers are known to be linked to specific genes. The presence of these genes doesn't guarantee that cancer will develop, but the incidence of cancer is much higher in people who have these genes. For example, mutations in the genes BRCA1 and BRCA2 have been linked to an increase in the incidence of breast and ovarian cancers. These genes are classified as tumor suppressor genes and, when they function improperly, they allow tumors to form more readily than in people who do not have these mutations.[10]

Other cancers associated with genetic mutations are retinoblastoma, a cancer of the retina of the eye: cancers of the lung, prostate, colon, bladder, and stomach: and certain forms of leukemia. Of course, there are other causes of these forms of cancer, but the question arises as to whether genes actually play an underlying role in the development of these cancers in some people and not in others.

Drug manufacturers are beginning to focus on cancer treatment drugs that are directed against the targets of misexpressed proteins produced as a result of genetic mutations. Drugs such as imatinib (Gleevec) actually block the action of abnormal proteins that signal cancer cells to multiply.

OBESITY

Obesity has been on the increase in the United States since the 1990s. Although often linked with coronary artery disease, high blood pressure, diabetes, and several other conditions, it has also been shown that it is associated with an increased risk of breast, endometrial, colon, kidney, and esophageal cancers.

One of the main reasons that obesity is linked to breast cancer is that detection of a lump in the breast is easier in a thin woman than in an obese one. This means that a developing tumor may be detected in an earlier stage in a thinner woman. As for colon cancer, it has been suggested that obese individuals have higher levels of insulin or insulin-related growth factors, both of which may promote tumor development.[11]

ENVIRONMENTAL TOXINS

Exposure to toxic wastes, toxic chemicals in the workplace and the environment, and certain chemicals found in foods and cosmetics have been associated with the development of different cancers.[12] Currently, there are approximately 50 million chemicals known and, unfortunately, scientists are unfamiliar with the biological effects of the majority of these substances. Some of these products fall into categories such as inorganic and organic chemicals, petrochemicals, agrochemicals (used in farming), fragrances and flavors and

Table 1.2 Cancers Diagnosed in the United States with the Greatest Frequency: Annual Rates		
Cancer Type	Estimated New Cases	Estimated Deaths
Bladder	70,980	14,330
Breast (Female; Male)	192,370; 1,910	40,170; 440
Colon and Rectal (Combined)	146,970	49,920
Endometrial	42,160	7,780
Kidney (Renal Cell) Cancer	49,096	11,033
Leukemia (All)	44,790	21,870
Lung (Including Bronchus)	219,440	159,390
Melanoma	68,720	8,650
Non-Hodgkin's Lymphoma	65,980	19,500
Pancreatic	42,470	35,240
Prostate	192,280	27,360
Skin (Nonmelanoma)	More than 1,000,000	Less than 1,000
Thyroid	37,200	1,630

Source: National Cancer Institute. "Common Cancer Types." Updated May 7, 2009. URL: http://www.cancer.gov/cancertopics/commoncancers. Accessed on September 24, 2009.

numerous others. Only some of the chemicals that humans are exposed to have been definitively linked to an increased cancer risk.

For example, **nitrosamines**, chemicals formed by the curing of meats such as bacon and ham, and polycyclic aromatic hydrocarbons, chemicals formed when foods are smoked or barbecued, have been shown to be carcinogenic. In addition, **heterocyclic amines**, formed when foods are fried at high temperatures, are also linked with an increase in cancer.[13]

Environmental toxins also play a role in causing cancer. For example, **formaldehyde** is found in building materials, pressed-wood products, cigarette smoke, and fuel-burning appliances. Benzene, a commonly found paint thinner and industrial cleaning agent, has been linked to the development of leukemia and serious blood diseases.[14]

VIRUSES

Certain viruses have been linked to the development of cancers. Of particular importance are human papillomavirus (HPV) and herpes simplex virus type 2 (HSV2). There are more than 100 different related human papillomaviruses. Many are harmless, but four types in particular are associated with cervical cancer. In 2006, the U.S. Food and Drug Administration (FDA) approved a vaccine named Gardasil that protects women against types 6, 11, 16 and 18, those that are most associated with this form of cancer. HSV2 has been linked to cervical cancer as well. However, it appears that it will only increase the risks if the patient is concurrently infected with HPV. The study showed that women infected with HSV2 alone had no increase in the occurrence of cervical cancer.[15]

There are other viruses that have been suggested as causes of different cancers. Hepatitis B and hepatitis C (HBV and HCV) have been linked to liver cancer, Epstein-Barr virus (EBV) has been linked to Burkitt's lymphoma, Hodgkin's lymphoma, and nasopharyngeal carcinoma, Kaposi's sarcoma herpesvirus, HPV5, HPV8 and HPV17, and skin cancer, retrovirus (human T-cell lymphotropic virus, HTLV2), and hairy cell leukemia, HTLV1, and adult T-cell leukemia/lymphoma.[16]

2
The History of Anticancer Drugs

The year was 2600 B.C. in ancient Egypt. Amunet, a middle-aged woman married to Thoth, a local architect, noticed a lump in her right breast. It was about as small as a green pea, but she was concerned as she had never noticed it before. After discussing it with her husband, she decided to pay a visit to Setmetnanch, a local physician with an excellent reputation as a healer.

After examining the lump, Setmetnanch told Amunet that he believed it to be a cancerous tumor. Not much was understood about cancer in those days, but people knew that it was a fatal disease. Amunet asked if there was any treatment that might save her life.

Setmetnanch felt that surgical removal of the tumor might help the situation, but he decided to start treatment chemically to see if that might reduce the tumor and help his patient avoid surgery. He mixed together a combination of castor oil, barley, and pigs' ears and applied the concoction to the skin of the breast directly over the lump. He told Amunet to take this mixture home and apply it every day until it ran out, then come back to see him.

WHERE DID IT ALL BEGIN?

It appears that the ancient Egyptians were the first to document their use of herbals and other ingredients to treat many maladies. In the 1800s, papyrus scrolls dating back to about 1600 B.C. were discovered by George Ebers and Edwin Smith. The scrolls, named for their discoverers, contain a wealth of information. For example, the Edwin Smith papyrus contains references to surgical procedures used by Egyptian physicians. The George Ebers papyrus details more than 700 recipes for various medicines.[1]

Quite a while later, the Romans in 300 B.C. were known to use ginger root to treat skin cancer and red clover and autumn crocus to fight other forms of the disease. More recently, in the years leading up to and including the medieval era, caustic alkaline solutions, arsenic, and zinc were used to treat various forms of cancer. In the nineteenth century, Robert Bentley, a researcher in London in 1861, discovered that the mayapple (*Podophyllum peltatum*) had a chemical in it that could fight tumors. Approximately 20 years later, researchers found that this chemical substance was picropodophyllin, a white crystalline substance that also worked as a **cathartic**. In 1946 researchers discovered that a combination of chemicals (picropodophyllin and picropodophyllic acid [also found in the mayapple], called podophyllotoxin) interfered with cell division and inhibited tumor growth.[2]

In 1893 Dr. William Coley used bacterial toxins to treat sarcoma in humans. Based on his observations, he deduced that a fever seemed to help reduce the size of tumors. He used the bacterial toxins from the disease **erysipelas**, which is caused by *Streptococcus pyogenes*, the bacteria that cause strep throat. Called Coley's toxins, it was injected into a patient who had tonsil and throat cancer. The cancer improved tremendously and the patient lived another eight and a half years.[3] Doctors in some foreign countries are still using Coley's toxins to treat cancers.[4]

The true beginning of modern cancer chemotherapy arrived in the 1940s when Louis Goodman and Alfred Gilman used mustine, a compound related to mustard gas, to treat non-Hodgkin's lymphoma with some success. From this point on, the drive to create new and more effective chemotherapeutic agents became the goal of many pharmaceutical companies.

Following World War II, another class of drugs was developed to combat cancer. After the discovery of folic acid by Lucy Wills in 1937, Dr. Sidney Farber investigated the effects of this vitamin on patients with acute lymphoblastic leukemia. In 1948 he found that by using folate analogs—drugs that blocked the function of folate-requiring enzymes—he could bring about remissions in children with acute lymphoblastic leukemia.[5] The first two

Figure 2.1 The two pharmacologists, Alfred Gilman (left) and Louis Goodman, who were hired by the U.S. Department of Defense to determine whether chemical warfare agents could be used therapeutically to treat cancer. They also wrote a textbook on pharmacology that has been widely used in medical schools for many years.   *(National Cancer Institute)*

analogs used were aminopterin and amethopterin (currently used under the name methotrexate). Unfortunately, the remissions didn't last long, but the concept was proven to be a sound one.

Farber was ridiculed by his colleagues who believed that leukemia was incurable. It took 10 years before their beliefs were shown to be mistaken when Drs. Roy Hertz and Min Chiu Li, working at the National Cancer Institute, used methotrexate to treat choriocarcinoma, a tumor that originates in the placenta.[6] This was the first use of the drug to treat a solid tumor. The drug was tested again by Dr. Joseph Burchenal, with Farber's help, at Memorial Sloan-Kettering Cancer Center with equal success.

Interfering with cell division, an approach that seemed quite logical in light of the fact that cancer cells divide at an accelerated rate, appeared to be an excellent approach to treating cancers. Burchenal, following his success with methotrexate, wanted to move in another direction to treat cancer. He and his team developed purine analogs that also worked against leukemia. The most effective was 6-mercaptopurine (6-MP).

Figure 2.2 Dr. Sidney Farber, who helped to create a class of anticancer drugs known as antifolates. These medicines were used to bring about remissions in children with acute lymphoblastic leukemia. *(National Library of Medicine)*

Following Burchenal's success, Eli Lilly and Company, a pharmaceutical manufacturer, discovered that a plant called Madagascar periwinkle (*Vinca rosea*) could also yield chemicals capable of inhibiting cell division.

A NEW APPROACH

Even though limited, these successes caused many scientists to believe that an approach using a combination of chemotherapeutic agents would be more successful in treating the various forms of cancer. This attack, known as combination chemotherapy, is based on the belief that two or more anti-cancer drugs may be used together to improve the effectiveness of each. This is known as a symbiotic approach to treatment.

In 1963 Drs. Vincent DeVita and George Canellos, working at the National Cancer Institute, used a combination of drugs to treat lymphomas. The drugs, 6-MP (Purinethol), vincristine (Oncovin), Methotrexate, and Prednisone, together became known as the POMP regimen.

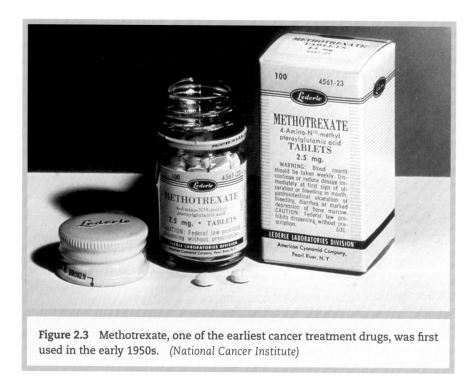

Figure 2.3 Methotrexate, one of the earliest cancer treatment drugs, was first used in the early 1950s. *(National Cancer Institute)*

In 1965 three cancer researchers, James Holland, Emil Frei, and Emil Freirich, wanted to improve on the POMP regimen and developed the MOPP regimen. They showed that the combination of nitrogen mustard, vincristine (Oncovin), procarbazine, and Prednisone could cure patients with Hodgkin's and non-Hodgkin's lymphomas. Following the success of these two regimens, researchers have continued to try different combinations of chemotherapy.[7] Some of these have brought about more damage than good, but in the long run, many new combinations have been useful in treating different forms of cancer.

ADJUVANT THERAPY

In a great number of cases of cancer, chemotherapy alone is not sufficient to bring about a cure or, in many cases, even a reduction in tumor size. This problem brought about the idea that **adjuvant therapy** might be an effective means of reducing or eliminating the rate of recurrence of cancers following surgical removal of the tumor or tumors. It was found that smaller tumors responded better to chemotherapy than did larger tumors. Adjuvant therapy involves using chemotherapy to remove remaining cells after the tumor has been surgically removed.

Adjuvant therapy was first used successfully by Dr. Emil Frei III in 1970 when he used high doses of methotrexate to prevent the recurrence of osteosarcoma after surgical removal of the primary tumor. Somewhat later, researchers used 5-fluorouracil, a drug that inhibits DNA synthesis, as an adjuvant in treating colon cancer. Further research done by Dr. Bernard Fisher in the United States and Dr. Gianni Bonadonna in Italy showed that adjuvant chemotherapy was very successful in extending survival time following complete surgical removal of breast tumors.[8]

ANOTHER PATHWAY

Prior to the developments noted above, another approach to chemotherapy was being investigated in 1956 by Dr. C. Gordon Zubrod, the director of the Division of Cancer Treatment at the National Cancer Institute. He felt that natural plant and marine sources could be used to find new drugs to treat cancer. At the time this was considered a novel approach to treatment,

Figure 2.4 Dr. C. Gordon Zubrod, former director of the Division of Cancer Treatment at the National Cancer Institute, whose desire to find anticancer drugs derived from natural sources, such as the Pacific yew tree, led to the development of taxanes and campothecins. *(National Cancer Institute)*

but he was successful in helping to create two anticancer drugs derived from plants.

Paclitaxel (Taxol) was discovered 23 years after Zubrod's efforts began and was used to treat ovarian cancer beginning in 1987. The drug interferes with mitosis and is found in the bark of the Pacific yew tree.

Another naturally derived anticancer drug was also developed thanks to Zubrod's efforts. Camptothecin is derived from a Chinese tree (*Camptotheca acuminata*), a member of the tupelo family known in China as *Xi Chu* ("happy tree"). This chemical inhibits the unwinding of DNA. Unfortunately, it can cause kidney damage, so it was not effective against tumors in early clinical trials because the dosages had to be very small. However, scientists were able to create a more stable form of the drug called irinotecan (Camptosar), which was approved for use in 1994 to treat colon, ovarian, and lung cancers.

A LUCKY ACCIDENT

In 1965 Dr. Barnett Rosenberg, working at Michigan State University, was attempting to determine the effects that an electrical field would have on the

Figure 2.5 Dr. Barnett Rosenberg, discoverer of cisplatin (*crystals shown*), a platinum-based compound used to treat solid cancerous tumors. *(National Cancer Institute)*

growth of the bacteria *Escherichia coli*. Although successful, it turned out that the inhibition of bacterial division that Rosenberg observed was caused, not by the electrical field, but by an electrolysis product of the platinum electrode.[9] The product was cisplatin, a platinum-based compound that damages DNA in cells, causing the cell to attempt to repair the damage. When this repair is unsuccessful, the cell activates the process of apoptosis (essentially "programmed" cell death). Rosenberg had his original success in treating sarcomas artificially implanted in rats. From there further research was carried out and derivatives of cisplatin were created that treated several types of cancer, particularly testicular cancer. The drug was approved for use in 1978 by the FDA.

ANOTHER CLASS OF DRUGS

Because of the widespread incidence of cancers throughout the world and the significant death rate associated with these cancers, researchers continued to seek out new classes of drugs that might work even better than older ones against different types of cancers. At the Southern Research Institute in Birmingham, Alabama, Dr. John Montgomery and his team synthesized nitrosoureas in 1963. These are alkylating agents that act similarly to the camptothecins in that they interfere with the unwinding of DNA. Their initial work showed that 1-methyl-1-nitrosourea worked well against leukemia in mice when implanted into the membrane that lines the abdominal cavity. It showed minimal activity, however, against two solid tumors, adenocarcinoma and sarcoma.[10]

Montgomery's success spurred him and his team to look for more compounds that could be used to treat cancers. They developed fludarabine, a chemical in the class of purine analogs (chemicals that resemble purines). Fludarabine inhibits DNA synthesis because it inhibits three enzymes (**DNA polymerase**, **ribonucleotide reductase** and **DNA primase)** needed for this process. It is particularly useful against B-cell chronic lymphocytic leukemia (CLL).[11]

HORMONES MAY PLAY A ROLE

More than 100 years ago, researchers showed that removing the ovaries of women suffering with breast cancer increased their survival rate. Today it is noted that women who have had their ovaries removed early in life have a far lower incidence of breast cancer than women who retain their ovaries. In fact, studies have shown that women with breast cancer have higher levels of estrogen in their blood.[12]

Along the same lines, when other treatments fail, many doctors perform surgical castration (orchiectomy, orchidectomy) to treat prostate cancer in men. The removal of the testicles lowers the levels of the hormone testosterone which seems to fuel the growth of prostate cancer in many cases. Of course, this procedure is permanent. Some men opt for chemical castration which employs anti-testosterone medications to lower the hormone's levels in the blood. If warranted, this procedure may be halted, thus allowing a return to normal levels of testosterone.

The drug tamoxifen (Nolvadex) was developed in the mid-1970s to treat and prevent various forms of breast cancer. It is classified as a selective estrogen receptor modulator (SERM), meaning that it blocks the estrogen receptor sites (proteins) on breast cancer cells that require estrogen to grow. Tamoxifen is used to treat early-stage breast cancer and metastatic breast cancer. It is also used as an adjuvant therapy after surgical removal of tumors to help prevent their recurrence. In addition, it has been used since the turn of the twenty-first century as a preventive measure in women who are at high risk for developing breast cancer.[13]

WHEN GENES ARE INVOLVED

Another approach to treating cancer involves getting down to the genetic level. This form of treatment is known as **targeted therapy**. Scientists have known for some time that chronic myelogenous leukemia (CML) is caused by a chromosomal translocation that leads to the development of an abnormal protein called kinase Bcr-Abl. Also known as the Philadelphia chromosome, it is identified by an abnormally short chromosome number 22 where the major part of the long arm has been translocated to chromosome number 9.

In the late 1990s Dr. Brian Druker and his team developed imatinib mesylate (Gleevec), a drug designed to inhibit kinase Bcr-Abl—an enzyme that leads to uncontrolled growth of leukemia cells. The drug was so successful in treating CML that 90% of those afflicted achieved complete remission. It is also used to treat patients with gastrointestinal stromal tumors (GIST) and several other rare forms of cancer.

WORKING WITH THE IMMUNE SYSTEM

Another approach to treating certain forms of cancer is to utilize antibodies to destroy cancer cells. The use of monoclonal antibodies is how this is accomplished. These antibodies are specific for one target antigen (usually a protein that stimulates an immune response) and are all clones of each other.

In 1997 a drug called rituximab (Rituxan and MabThera) was approved by the FDA to treat B-cell non-Hodgkin's lymphoma. It works by binding to CD20, a protein complex on the surface of B-cells. These are one of several types of white blood cells used by the body's immune system. They are referred to as memory cells and produce antibodies. The binding of rituximab to the surface of these cells brings about apoptosis.[14]

Given the continued widespread occurrence of so many forms of cancer, ongoing research aimed at developing new chemotherapy agents is taking place worldwide. Pharmaceutical companies, university laboratories, hospital research facilities, and many other groups are moving forward with research projects aimed at developing new drugs and new approaches to therapy. This is extremely important as cancer continually proves that it is very hard to beat.

3

Which Drugs Are Used to Treat Specific Forms of Cancer?

Ted had worked hard all year and was definitely looking forward to his vacation with the family. They were planning to go to Denver to see the sights and do some skiing in the Rocky Mountains. He had been feeling tired for the past few weeks, but he attributed this to the long hours he had been putting in at the office and the fact that he wasn't sleeping more than five hours each night so he could get to work early in the morning.

The big day arrived, and Ted and his family left their home in Miami Beach and boarded the plane for Denver. Everyone was eager to get there and start having fun—and the adults were looking forward to some well-deserved relaxation time.

The plane arrived in Denver and the family couldn't wait to get to the hotel, settle in, maybe do some swimming and go to dinner at a fancy restaurant. Spirits were high and smiles were on everybody's face. But within 24 hours, Ted noticed that, instead of feeling rested and recharged by the change of scene, he was becoming increasingly tired and had difficulty walking for any length of time or doing any type of exercise. He was perplexed and could not figure out why he should be feeling worse than he did while he was back home with all of the responsibilities and time at work. He continued to feel tired and weak, so his wife took him to the hospital.

The first test performed at the hospital was a blood test that included a full chemistry panel and a complete blood count (CBC). This would take a few hours to analyze, so Ted and his family waited anxiously for the results.

The doctor returned with the results and had a serious look on his face. Ted was suffering from acute myeloid (myelogenous) leukemia (AML), the most common form of leukemia seen in adults. One of its effects is a reduced red blood count. This was the cause of Ted's extreme exhaustion. At the elevated altitude of Denver, the oxygen levels in the atmosphere are lower than they are at sea level in Miami Beach. Ted's body could not adequately perform in a reduced oxygen atmosphere. The family cut their vacation short and flew back to Miami Beach to get Ted the treatment he needed.

THE MANY FORMS OF CANCER

Cancer is a disease that is characterized by dedifferentiation of cells. That is, they lose their ability to function in the manner they were designed for and become more like the original stem cells that they arose from. Cancer cells display invasion of surrounding areas, uncontrolled growth, and, at times, metastasis. Cancers are usually seen in the form of a tumor, but, as in Ted's case, leukemias and lymphomas are considered cancers of the blood or bone marrow and are not associated with tumor growth.

Once a tumor has been detected using a diagnostic procedure such as an X-ray, computerized axial tomography (CAT) scan, or magnetic resonance imaging (MRI) a biopsy may be taken and analyzed in order to identify the specific type of cancer. Once this is done, if a treatment exists, the oncologist (a doctor who treats cancers) will recommend the proper treatment. It might be radiation therapy, surgery, chemotherapy, or a combination of these. The recommendation must be based on personal experience and a thorough understanding of the research that has been done on treating the particular type of tumor.

In cases of nontumor cancers such as leukemia, lymphoma, and multiple myeloma, a blood sample is taken in order to confirm a diagnosis. Examination of the blood sample will let the pathologist identify the specific types of cancer cells present. Treatment may be administered in any one or a combination of forms. Chemotherapy in the form of a single drug or a combination of drugs is often used for these cancers. In addition, radiation may be used as well as bone marrow transplantation.

Cancerous tumors occur in many different forms associated with numerous physical characteristics. The National Cancer Institute lists 218 different types of cancer that affect humans. Many of these are extremely rare, but all deserve the NCI's attention. This is why they are included in the extensive list made available to the public on the NCI's Web site.[1]

THE GOAL OF CANCER CHEMOTHERAPY

One may consider cancer cells to be "supercells." That is, they are able to do several things that normal cells cannot do. This gives them the capability of surviving in the face of adverse conditions. For example, they are able to put certain biological mechanisms into play that will assure them of a long and destructive life. Additionally, they are known to make changes in their biochemistry that allow them to resist many chemotherapeutic agents and adapt to toxic environments.

Cancer chemotherapy is designed to shrink primary tumors, slow tumor growth, and kill cancer cells that may have spread (metastasized) to other parts of the body. In addition, relieving the signs and symptoms of cancer is extremely important if a person with cancer is to return to a normal lifestyle. This is certainly a logical approach to treatment, but there are roadblocks along the way.

One of the major problems associated with the use of many of the older cancer chemotherapy drugs is that, although the drugs may work to interfere with some part of the cancer cell's life cycle, they cannot differentiate between cancer cells and normal cells. This means that they will attack normal cells and cause many of the typical side effects associated with cancer chemotherapy. These side effects include nausea and vomiting, anemia due to a reduction in the production of red blood cells, a reduction in the number of white blood cells (used by the immune system) and hair loss. Another difficulty is that cancer cells, because of their rapid metabolism and altered biochemistry, often become resistant to the medications that once were effective. Additionally, many anticancer drugs target only specific types of cancer cells, and if more than one type exists in a tumor, those that are not targeted will continue to do damage. Some of the newer cancer treatment drugs, as described previously, are able to target the specific wrongly-produced proteins formed due to genetic mutations, thus protecting normal cells. These drugs are also associated with side effects, but they are usually significantly reduced in comparison with those brought about by the older drugs that were aimed at "poisoning" cancer cells.

When treating cancers, doctors aim at achieving a complete remission of the disease. This is defined as no signs of the cancer on diagnostic tests (X-rays, CAT scans, MRIs, blood tests) and physical examination. A partial remission is achieved with a 50% or greater reduction in tumor size.[2] The majority of remissions are partial. This reduction may be detected in several ways. One would be by using a blood, urine, or tissue test to detect specific biomarkers that might be released by a cancerous tumor. Examples of these markers include Carcinoembryonic Antigen (CEA) in cases of cancers located in the gastrointestinal tract, ovaries, lungs, pancreas, and breast; Cancer Antigen 15-3 (CA 15-3), found in advanced cases of breast cancer; and Cancer Antigen 125 (CA 125), detectable in cases of ovarian cancer.

Another means of determining if a particular chemotherapy regimen is working is by measurements of a tumor taken using X-rays, CAT scans, or MRI. Although these diagnostic tools are used initially to detect a tumor, they are also useful in following up to see if the size of the tumor has been reduced by a particular form of chemotherapy or radiation therapy. Measurements taken before and after treatment will reveal the degree of success achieved.

WHICH DRUGS ARE USED TO TREAT DIFFERENT FORMS OF CANCER?

There are many different drugs available to treat the numerous forms of cancer seen among humans and animals. Considering that there are at least 218 different types of cancer, it would be impossible to itemize all of the treatment regimens used to combat the various cancers. Here the most common forms of cancer will be discussed briefly along with chemotherapeutic treatment options.

BASAL CELL CARCINOMA

At the bottom of the epidermis (the outer layer of the skin) is a layer of cells called the basal layer. This is the site for the development of basal cell carcinomas, the most common form of skin cancer. In fact, 75% of all skin cancers are of this type. Although they rarely metastasize and the fatality rate associated with them is very low, they may still be very destructive locally and should not be ignored. Most cases occur on the head and neck.[3]

Most basal cell carcinomas are caused by excessive exposure to ultraviolet radiation—too much exposure to sunlight or tanning booths. At times, the cancer may develop soon after intense exposure, but there are also many cases that don't appear until years after the actual exposure. The true cause is damage to the cells' DNA by the ultraviolet light. Although this damage may be repaired in many cases, often some of it escapes repair and a carcinoma develops.

Treatment for these cancers is based on the size and location of the lesion, the patient's age, general health, and preferences.[4] There are several methods, among them **electrodesiccation**, various methods of traditional surgery, **cryosurgery**, radiation, and topical chemotherapy. This last technique employs the use of skin creams that contain imiquimod or 5-fluorouracil. These will effectively destroy the cancer cells, but may be used only if the cancer is very superficial. Deeper carcinomas require one of the other methods noted.

BLADDER CANCER

Cancer of the urinary bladder is not an extremely common one. The National Cancer Institute estimated that there were approximately 71,000 new cases in the United States in 2009.[5] Some of the causes of bladder cancer include exposure to environmental toxins such as benzidine (used in making certain dyes and detecting blood), aniline dyes (synthetic organic dyes often made from coal tar), and chemicals used in leather treatment and paint production. In addition, smoking and parasitic infections of the bladder increase the risk of developing bladder cancer.

The course of therapy is determined by the degree of invasiveness of the tumor. Those that are superficial are often treated with simple removal of the tumor or removal combined with surgical resection of the bladder. In addition, the treating physician may feel that the use of neo-adjuvant chemotherapy is warranted. If the cancer is confined to the lining of the bladder, the patient might receive intravesical chemotherapy. This technique involves inserting a catheter into the urethra (the tube that allows passage of urine from the bladder) so the chemotherapy can be introduced directly into the bladder. The medicine remains there for a few hours and is then drained out again. This protects the rest of the body from exposure to the medication.

Figure 3.1 An oncology nurse administers cancer treatment drugs to a patient by catheter. *(National Cancer Institute)*

Deeper cancers require more extensive surgical intervention. In addition to removing the tumor or tumors, the surgeon may have to remove a part of or the entire bladder (cystectomy). If the cancer has spread, a radical cystectomy may be performed. In a radical cystectomy the bladder and nearby organs and lymph nodes are removed. In most of these cases, the physician will also use neo-adjuvant chemotherapy aimed at destroying any remaining cancer cells.

Radiation is also an option that many doctors use to destroy bladder tumors and keep the cells from metastasizing. In some cases, radiation alone is effective in destroying the tumors. However, most doctors will also add chemotherapy to the treatment regimen.

Once again, the particular chemotherapeutic drug used will be determined by the extent of the cancer. Several agents are commonly used, including carboplatin, cisplatin, cyclophosphamide, doxorubicin, methotrexate, and vinblastine.

BONE CANCER

Primary bone cancers are those that arise within the bone. These do not include metastatic cancers that have traveled to bones from a distant site such as the bladder, prostate, breast, or lung. These types of cancer are rare and account for only 1% of all cancers.[6] Common types of primary bone cancer include osteosarcoma, chondrosarcoma, and the Ewing's sarcoma family of tumors (ESFTs).

Osteosarcoma (also known as osteogenic sarcoma) develops from osteoid tissue in the bone. This is bone tissue that exists prior to ossification (the actual laying down of bone cells). The disease is usually seen in the long bones of the arm and leg (particularly around the knee) in young people. In addition, it occurs more often in males than in females. It accounts for 20% of all primary bone cancers. These tumors often require surgical removal, and the oncologist frequently uses neo-adjuvant chemotherapy prior to surgery to treat the patient. In cases where tissue necrosis (death of cells or tissues due to injury or disease) is extensive, the chemotherapy regimen is continued after the surgery. The drugs most often used for this are cisplatin, adriamycin, methotrexate in combination with folinic acid, and a few others. The average five-year survival rate following surgery and chemotherapy is 65% to 70%.

Chondrosarcoma is a cancer that begins in cartilaginous tissue (the prefix "chondro" refers to cartilage). Hyaline cartilage is a type of cartilage found at the joint ends of bones (epiphysis). It occurs most frequently in the shoulder, the upper leg, the knee, and the pelvis between the hipbones. It is the second most common type of primary bone cancer. It is seen most often in patients between the ages of 50 and 70.

The primary treatment for this type of cancer is surgery. In fact, most oncologists won't use chemotherapy for chondrosarcomas as it is not very effective. However, if there is metastasis, chemotherapy may be employed to treat those areas where the cells have traveled. In addition, in advanced cases of chondrosarcoma a combination of radiation and chemotherapy might be used.

It has been found that, depending on the location of the tumor, different chemotherapeutic drugs are helpful in bringing about a complete remission. Some of these are used as neo-adjuvants and others as adjuvants.[7] Drugs associated with the greatest success rates are cyclophosphamide, cisplatin, adriamycin, ifosfamide, methotrexate, and etoposide.

The Ewing's sarcoma family of tumors is a group of small, round-cell tumors that arise most often in the pelvis, chest wall, arms, or legs. It is not uncommon for cells from these tumors to metastasize to the lungs, bone marrow, or other bones. In more than 85% of cases, there is a genetic translocation between chromosomes 11 and 22.[8]

These tumors are the second most common type of bone cancer in both adolescents and children, with approximately 50% of cases seen in individuals between the ages of 10 and 20. There are approximately 200 new cases diagnosed each year in the United States. Two-thirds of the children diagnosed with localized cases will survive. Once metastasis has occurred, however, less than 30% survive.

It appears that surgery and/or radiation therapy for localized tumors is not very effective in preventing tumor recurrence. Therefore, oncologists use chemotherapy to ensure destruction of cancer cells at not only the original site but also those that have metastasized. The most commonly used chemotherapeutic drugs are vincristine, doxorubicin, cyclophosphamide, ifosfamide, and etoposide.

BRAIN TUMORS

There are many different types of brain tumors because there are many different types of cells in the brain. Half of the brain is made up of neurons. These are the cells that conduct electrical impulses throughout the body in order to bring sensory information to the brain and carry motor impulses to muscles, glands, and organs so specific actions can take place. The other half of the brain is made up of cells called **neuroglia (glial cells)**. These include **astrocytes**, **oligodendrocytes**, **ependymal cells**, and **microglia**.

Brain tumors arise in any of these cells and also in lymphatic tissue, blood vessels, cranial nerves that exit the brain, pineal and pituitary glands, skull bones, and the meninges (three layers of connective tissue that protect the brain and spinal cord). The National Cancer Institute estimated that there were more than 22,000 new cases of brain cancer in the United States in 2009 and nearly 13,000 deaths.[9]

The most common malignant brain tumors arise in the glial cells. (It's not uncommon for medical professionals to see benign [noncancerous] tumors, but these are not discussed in this book.) Astrocytomas, those that develop

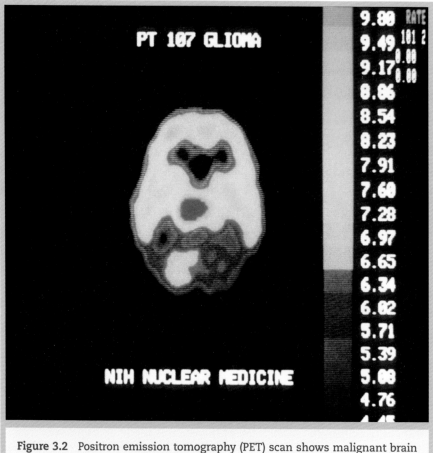

Figure 3.2   Positron emission tomography (PET) scan shows malignant brain tumor (in red).   *(National Cancer Institute)*

from astrocytes, may grow anywhere in the brain or spinal cord. In adults they are usually found in the cerebrum, the main portion of the brain, which is responsible for thinking, reasoning, interpretation of information, and many other functions. In children they are most often located in the brain stem (the region that connects the spinal cord to the brain), the cerebrum, and the cerebellum (the structure responsible for balance and muscle coordination).

Ependymomas, tumors that develop in ependymal cells, are located in the ventricles of the brain, where the ependymal cells are responsible for the production of cerebrospinal fluid that aids in brain and spinal cord function.

Additionally, these tumors may be found in the spinal cord. They are most common in childhood and adolescence.

Oligodendrogliomas arise from oligodendrocytes, the cells responsible for the production of myelin in the central nervous system (brain and spinal cord). Myelin insulates nerves so that the electrical impulses can travel rapidly. Oligodendrogliomas occur most often in middle-aged adults.

Medulloblastomas are tumors that do not begin in glial cells. These tumors apparently develop from primitive or developing nerve cells that were present during embryological development. These cells should not be present after birth. If they remain, they may be likely to develop into tumors. They most often arise in children in the cerebellum and are more common in boys than in girls.

How does the oncologist choose which type of chemotherapy to use to treat a brain tumor? He or she takes into consideration the patient's age, physical condition, typical side effects associated with the different drugs, type of cancer, and a number of other factors. Typically, the drugs are used following surgery and/or radiation therapy and include carboplatin, vincristine, thioguanine, lomustine (CCNU), temozolomide, and procarbazine hydrochloride.[10]

BREAST CANCER

Breast cancer usually arises in the ducts that carry milk to the nipples and in the lobules, which are the glands that make the milk. It occurs in both men and women, but only about 1% of cases are seen in men. The National Cancer Institute estimated that there were more than 192,000 cases in women and almost 2,000 cases in men in the United States in 2009, resulting in more than 40,000 deaths among females and more than 400 deaths among males.[11] The causes include smoking, genetics, moderate intake of alcohol, exposure to chemicals and hormones, never having been pregnant, early onset of menstruation, and several others.

In most cases of breast cancer, surgery is usually the first treatment. The kind of surgery used is determined by the stage of the cancer, how the cancer "behaves," and what the patient is comfortable with as far as long-term goals are concerned. In many cases, a lumpectomy is all that is needed. This conserves the breast by removing only the tumor and a small amount of surrounding tissue. In other cases, a mastectomy is necessary. This involves removal

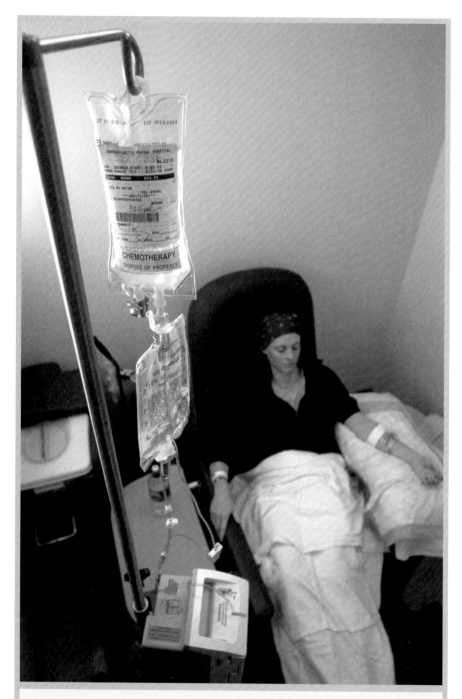

Figure 3.3 A cancer patient receives cancer treatment drugs administered intravenously. (©*Photo Researchers, Inc.*)

of all of the breast tissue. However, thanks to many medical advances, the underlying muscles are usually left intact.

In some cases, the cancer may spread beyond the breast into the axillary lymph nodes, in the armpit. If this occurs, these nodes must be removed along with the cancerous tissue. This removal may be done along with either the lumpectomy or the mastectomy, depending on the specific situation.

After surgery, many oncologists recommend radiation therapy. This is particularly true in patients who have undergone lumpectomies. The rationale is that the radiation will destroy any cancer cells left behind. This is usually done when the cancer is in an early stage, is small, is located in one site only, or when the margins surrounding the tumor are clear. The same holds true following mastectomies. In these cases, though, the indications are somewhat different, particularly because a mastectomy is generally performed when the cancer is more advanced. In such situations the tumor is usually greater than 5 centimeters, it has invaded the lymphatic system locally, it has invaded the skin, and several lymph nodes show the presence of cancerous cells.

Chemotherapy is often used to treat breast cancer regardless of the stage it is in. The therapy is used as both an adjuvant (after surgery) to kill undetected cells that might have metastasized, or as a neoadjuvant (before surgery to shrink the tumor). It has been found that combinations of chemotherapeutic drugs are most effective in treating breast cancer. A number of combinations are used based on the patient's state of health, stage of the cancer, and type of cancer. Numerous clinical studies have been performed that have enabled doctors to choose which combination is best for a particular individual. The combinations are referred to with abbreviations and are summarized in Table 3.1.

CERVICAL CANCER

Cervical cancer occurs in the cervix, the portion of the uterus that connects it with the vagina. This is a slow-growing cancer that is often not associated with symptoms until it is advanced. However, an annual Pap test (named for its creator Dr. Georgios Papanicolaou) can detect the earliest changes in the cells of the cervix that are associated with the future development of cancer. This form of cancer is almost always caused by human papillomavirus (HPV). The National Cancer Institute estimated that there were more than 11,000 new cases and more than 4,000 deaths associated with this cancer in the United States in 2009.[12]

Table 3.1 Chemotherapy Combinations for Treating Breast Cancer	
CMF	cyclophosphamide, methotrexate, and 5-fluorouracil
CAF	cyclophosphamide, doxorubicin (Adriamycin), and 5-fluorouracil
AC	doxorubicin (Adriamycin) and cyclophosphamide
EC	epirubicin and cyclophosphamide
TAC	docetaxel (Taxotere), doxorubicin (Adriamycin), and cyclophosphamide
ACT	doxorubicin (Adriamycin) and cyclophosphamide followed by paclitaxel (Taxol) or docetaxel (Taxotere)
ACMF	doxorubicin (Adriamycin), followed by CMF
CEF	cyclophosphamide, epirubicin, and 5-fluorouracil (this may be followed by docetaxel)
TC	docetaxel (Taxotere) and cyclophosphamide
TCH	docetaxel (Taxotere), carboplatin, and Herceptin (trastuzumab) for HER2/neu positive tumors

Source: American Cancer Society. "Detailed Guide: Breast Cancer Chemotherapy." URL: http://www.cancer.org/docroot/CRI/content/CRI_2_4_4X_Chemotherapy_5.asp?rnav=cri. Accessed on November 12, 2009.

The method of treatment that the doctor decides on is based on several factors. These include the size of the tumor, the patient's age, whether the patient wants to have children (or any more children), and what stage the cancer is in at the time of the examination. If a woman is pregnant when the cancer is diagnosed, the method of treatment will be based on the stage of the cancer and of the pregnancy.

One of the approaches to treating cervical cancer is surgery. A number of different procedures are used depending on what the doctor feels will be appropriate. A cone biopsy may be performed to simply diagnose or to actually treat the cancer. In this procedure, a cone-shaped piece of tissue is removed and analyzed. If the analysis shows that the section taken is larger than the actual cancer, no further surgery is needed. A total hysterectomy may be performed, in which the uterus and cervix are removed. In some cases the doctor will feel that a more extensive surgery is needed based on possible spread of cancerous cells and will perform a total hysterectomy with salpingo-oophorectomy. In this procedure, the uterus, cervix, ovaries, and fallopian tubes (the tubes that carry the egg from the ovary to the uterus) are removed. In more serious cases, when metastasis has occurred and the surrounding tissues are affected, a radical hysterectomy is performed. This includes removal of the uterus and cervix, the ovaries, the fallopian tubes, part of the vagina, and some of the tissues surrounding the area. In addition, some of the local lymph nodes may be removed. In less severe cases, cryosurgery may be performed. This involves the use of an instrument that freezes and destroys abnormal tissue. It is used most often in cases of carcinoma in situ (cancer isolated to one small site). Laser surgery may also be used when a small area is affected.

Cervical cancer may also be treated with radiation therapy. The actual method used depends on the type and stage of the cancer being treated. These procedures include external radiation, in which the beam of radioactivity is aimed from the outside of the body toward the tumor, or internal radiation, in which the radioactive material is introduced into the body and placed at the site of the tumor via needles, "seeds" (radioactive pellets), wires, or catheters.

Chemotherapy may be used to treat cervical cancer. The drugs most often used as a first line of defense are cisplatin, paclitaxel (Taxol), topotecan, ifosfamide, and fluorouracil (5-FU).[13] In addition, chemotherapy is often used in conjunction with radiation therapy. Some medications are given four hours prior to the radiation treatment, while others are given during the time period between radiation treatments. Although this method of treatment can improve the prognosis, it is also associated with an increase in negative side effects such as nausea and vomiting, fatigue, diarrhea, and low blood counts.

COLON AND RECTAL CANCER

The colon is another name for the large intestine. This is the lower portion of the digestive system and is approximately five feet long in the average adult. The terminal portion of the colon is the rectum, where feces are stored prior to defecation. The colon and rectum are common sites for the development of cancers. Most colon and rectal cancers are adenocarcinomas, tumors that begin in cells that make and release mucus and other fluids. The National Cancer Institute estimated that there were more than

106,000 cases of colon cancer and more than 40,000 cases of rectal cancer in the United States in 2009. In addition, the institute estimated that the two types of cancer caused a total of nearly 50,000 deaths in 2009.[14]

The usual treatment for these cancers is surgical resection of the region involved and removal of lymph nodes in the area. Adjuvant chemotherapy is used in many different situations, particularly when metastasis has occurred.

Table 3.2 Chemotherapy Combinations for Treating Advanced Colon and Rectal Cancers	
Arbeitsgemeinschaft Internische Onkologie (AIO) or German AIO regimen	folic acid, 5-FU, and irinotecan
CAPOX regimen	capecitabine plus oxaliplatin
Douillard regimen	folic acid, 5-FU, and irinotecan
FOLFOX4 regimen	oxaliplatin, leucovorin, and 5-FU (Oxaliplatin [85 mg/m²] administered as a 2-hour infusion on day 1; leucovorin [200 mg/m²] administered as a 2-hour infusion on day 1 and day 2; followed by a loading dose of 5-FU [400 mg/m²] IV bolus, then 5-FU [600 mg/m²] administered via ambulatory pump for a period of 22 hours on day 1 and day 2 every 2 weeks.)
FOLFOX6 regimen	oxaliplatin, leucovorin, and 5-FU (Oxaliplatin [85–100 mg/m²] administered as a 2-hour infusion on day 1; leucovorin [400 mg/m²] administered as a 2-hour infusion on day 1; followed by a loading dose of 5-FU [400 mg/m²] IV bolus on day 1, then 5-FU [2,400–3,000 mg/m²] administered via ambulatory pump for a period of 46 hours every 2 weeks.)
FOLFIRI regimen	folic acid, 5-FU, and irinotecan
FUFOX regimen	oxaliplatin, leucovorin, 5-FU
FUOX regimen	5-FU plus oxiplatin
IFL (or Saltz) regimen	irinotecan, 5-FU, and leucovorin
XELOX regimen	capecitabine plus oxaliplatin

Source: National Cancer Institute. "Stage IV and Recurrent Colon Cancer." URL: http://www.cancer.gov/cancertopics/pdq/treatment/colon/HealthProfessional/77.cdr#Section_77. Accessed on November 13, 2009.

A number of regimens using combinations of chemotherapeutic drugs have been developed to treat the more advanced stages of the disease. These are summarized in Table 3.2.

KAPOSI'S SARCOMA

This form of cancer is frequently found in patients with acquired immuno-deficiency syndrome (AIDS). In fact, it is considered an indicator disease for AIDS. It is not a very common form of cancer in the general population, but it has been known to occur more frequently in elderly men of the Mediterranean region and of eastern European descent as well as young individuals from sub-Saharan Africa. The reason for this is that the cancer is caused by human herpesvirus 8 (HHV8), which is widespread in these regions.[15] It occurs frequently in AIDS patients because their immune systems are severely suppressed by the human immunodeficiency virus (HIV) and they cannot fight off the HHV8 as easily as someone with a normal immune system can. It is also found in patients who have received transplanted organs because their immune systems are intentionally suppressed by medications to reduce the rejection of the transplanted organ.

Treatment for this form of cancer is more limited than for other forms. Surgery is not recommended because the edges of the surgical area most likely will have remaining cancer cells that will continue to spread. Surgery may be used when only a single lesion is present. Radiation therapy is used only when multiple lesions are present in several areas of the body.

Chemotherapy usually includes the anticancer drug paclitaxel. In addition, a combination drug therapy, which includes doxorubicin (Adriamycin), bleomicin, and vincristine (ABV), has been used with success. The cancer is usually found on the skin, but may also invade the lungs and gastrointestinal tract as well as many other parts of the body. The mean survival rate for AIDS-related Kaposi's sarcoma is 15–24 months without treatment for AIDS. However, with the increased use of drugs to combat AIDS, the survival rate has increased.[16]

LEUKEMIA AND LYMPHOMA

There are many different types of leukemia and lymphoma. Leukemia is a cancer of the blood that manifests as an abnormal production of blood cells in the circulation, particularly white blood cells (the cells that are normally part of the immune system). Lymphoma is a cancer of the lymphocytes, which are one of the five types of white blood cells. This leads to solid tumors of lymphoid cells that appear as masses in lymph nodes rather than remaining in the circulation.

The leukemias are classified as either acute or chronic. The acute forms are associated with a rapid overproduction of immature cells in the bone marrow. This activity replaces the normal production of healthy blood cells and requires immediate treatment as the continuing decrease in the numbers of healthy cells will quickly lead to death. This type of leukemia is most common in children.

Chronic leukemias are much slower to develop and go on for years. These are associated with an increase in the numbers of mature but abnormal white blood cells. These cells do not function properly, and eventually treatment must begin. Due to the slow development of this form of leukemia, treatment may not begin immediately and may be delayed until the disease is at a point where the maximum benefit from treatment may be achieved. This type of leukemia is most often seen in adults, although children may develop it as well.

The categories of acute and chronic leukemia are further divided into specific types. Acute leukemias include acute lymphoblastic leukemia (ALL) (lymphoblasts are the precursors to lymphocytes) and acute myelogenous leukemia (AML) (this involves all other white blood cells and platelets). Chronic leukemias include chronic lymphocytic leukemia (CLL) and chronic myelogenous leukemia (CML).

The treatment regimens for the different types of leukemia vary depending on which type is being treated and on the phase of treatment being applied. Radiation therapy is utilized when an area of bone is very painful, when there are a great number of abnormal cells and when a bone marrow transplant is pending. In the third case, the radiation will destroy bone marrow throughout the patient's body so that the donor bone marrow will be the only cells producing blood cells for the recipient. In addition, radiation is used to protect the brain from leukemia, particularly in children with ALL.

Chemotherapy for the different forms of leukemia varies from type to type of leukemia. Tables 3.3 and 3.4 delineate the treatment for ALL and AML. The primary treatment for AML is chemotherapy.

The treatment regimens for the chronic forms of leukemia are somewhat different than those for the acute forms. The reason is that patients with these

Table 3.3 Chemotherapy for Acute Lymphoblastic Leukemia		
Phase	Description	Agents
Remission induction	The aim of remission induction is to rapidly kill most tumor cells and get the patient into remission. This is defined as the presence of less than 5% leukemic blasts in the bone marrow, normal blood cells and absence of tumor cells from blood, and absence of other signs and symptoms of the disease.	Combination of predniso-lone or dexamethasone (in children), vincristine, as-paraginase, and daunoru-bicin (used in adult ALL) is used to induce remission.
Intensification	Intensification uses high doses of intravenous multidrug che-motherapy to further reduce tumor burden. Since cells in ALL sometimes penetrate the central nervous system (CNS), most protocols include deliv-ery of chemotherapy into the CNS fluid (termed intrathecal chemotherapy). Some can-cer treatment centers deliver the drug through an Ommaya reservoir (a device surgically placed under the scalp and used to deliver drugs to the CNS fluid and to extract CNS fluid for various tests). Other centers perform multiple lumbar punc-tures (spinal taps) as needed for testing and treatment delivery.	Typical intensification protocols use vincris-tine, cyclophosphamide, cytarabine, daunorubicin, etoposide, thioguanine, or mercaptopurine given as blocks in different combi-nations. For CNS protec-tion, intrathecal metho-trexate or cytarabine is usually used combined with or without cranio-spinal irradiation (the use of radiation therapy to the head and spine). Central nervous system relapse is treated with intrathecal administration of hydro-cortisone, methotrexate, and cytarabine.
Maintenance therapy	The aim of maintenance ther-apy is to kill any residual cell that was not killed by remission induction, and intensification regimens. Although such cells are few, they will cause relapse if not eradicated.	For this purpose, daily oral mercaptopurine, once weekly oral methotrexate, one monthly 5-day course of intravenous vincristine and oral corticosteroids are usually used. The length of maintenance therapy is 3 years for boys, 2 years for girls and adults.

Source: A.V. Hoffbrand, P.A.H. Moss, J.E. Pettit, Essential Haematology. Fifth edition. (Hobo-ken, N.J.: Blackwell, 2006).

Table 3.4 Chemotherapy for Acute Myeloblastic Leukemia		
Phase	Description	Agents
Induction	The goal of induction therapy is to achieve a complete remission by reducing the amount of leukemic cells to an undetectable level.	To bring on induction, it is customary to treat with cytarabine (ara-C) and an anthracycline (such as daunorubicin or idarubicin). Due to toxic side effects, this treatment is not offered to the very elderly.
Consolidation	The goal of consolidation therapy is to eliminate any residual undetectable disease and achieve a cure.	This therapy is used even when a complete remission has been achieved. The rationale for this is that there are still some leukemic cells remaining in the body, although they are undetectable. Cytarabine is the drug of choice for this therapy. It may be given with etoposide, daunomycin, and idarubicin. Stem cell transplantation is recommended in this phase as well.
Relapsed AML	For patients with relapsed AML, the only proven potentially curative therapy is a stem cell transplant, if one has not already been performed. Patients with relapsed AML who are not candidates for stem cell transplantation, or who have relapsed after a stem cell transplant, may be offered treatment in a clinical trial, as conventional treatment options are limited.	Because only 20%–30% of patients achieve successful long-term remission of AML with these treatments, stem cell transplantation is recommended in relapse cases. Gemtuzumab ozogamicin is used in the elderly who cannot tolerate high-dose chemotherapy. In addition, patients who have relapsed and are not candidates for a stem cell transplant are given clofarabine, farnesyl transferase inhibitors, decitabine, and inhibitors of multidrug-resistance protein MRD1.

Source: National Marrow Donor Program, "Acute Myelogenous Leukemia (AML)," http://www.marrow.org/PATIENT/Undrstnd_Disease_Treat/Lrn_about_Disease/AML/index.html#TreatmentOptionsforAcuteMyelogenousLeukemia (accessed August 24, 2010).

forms of leukemia can live for many years. In fact, it is not uncommon to provide no treatment at all in the early stages of these leukemias, but to merely watch the patient's progress and monitor his or her blood for significant changes. Treatment begins when changes start to affect the patient's quality of life. There appears to be no survival advantage in starting treatment early in the disease.

Treatment for chronic lymphocytic leukemia (CLL) often begins with chlorambucil or sometimes with fludarabine. Other drugs include alemtuzumab, rituximab, and combination therapies that appear to have a better response rate. These include FC (fludarabine with cyclophosphamide), FR (fludarabine with rituximab), FCR (fludarabine, cyclophosphamide, and rituximab) and CHOP (cyclophosphamide, doxorubicin [hydroxydoxorubicin], vincristine [Oncovin] and prednisolone).[17]

Chronic myelogenous leukemia (CML) is often associated with a chromosomal translocation known as the Philadelphia chromosome. This translocation includes the repositioning of genetic material between chromosomes 9 and 22.

In the past, treatment for CML included the use of antimetabolites (such as cytarabine and hydroxyurea), alkylating agents, interferon alfa 2b, and steroids. Now the treatment of choice is imatinib mesylate (Gleevec). This drug targets the tyrosine kinase fusion protein caused by the Philadelphia chromosome translocation, thus reducing or eliminating the production of abnormal blood cells.[18]

Lymphoma, as the name suggests, begins in the lymphocytes and develops into solid tumors in the lymphatic system. There are many types of lymphomas and the diseases associated with them will vary to some degree. The World Health Organization lists 43 different types of lymphomas divided into four categories. In 1832 Thomas Hodgkin published the first description of the lymphoma now named after him. Some forms will cause death in a short time; others may have little or no effect on an individual. It should be noted, however, that even the potentially fatal forms of lymphoma may respond well to treatment.

Hodgkin's lymphoma is one form of the many lymphomas. It is associated with a continuous spread of the disease from one lymph node group to the next and the presence of Reed-Sternberg cells (giant cells derived from B-lymphocytes). If left untreated, the lymphomas continue to spread and eventually invade organs. As the disease progresses, systemic signs develop. These may include weight loss, night sweats, back pain, spleen and

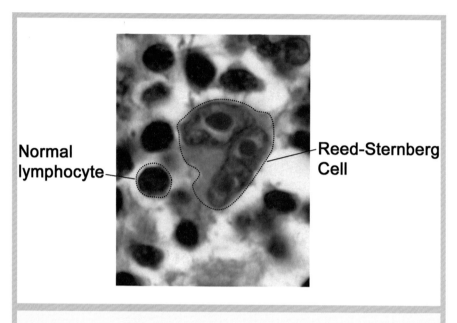

Figure 3.4 Photograph shows normal lymphocytes compared with a Reed-Sternberg cell, which are found in Hodgkin's lymphoma. Reed-Sternberg cells are large, abnormal lymphocytes that may contain more than one nucleus. *(National Cancer Institue)*

liver enlargement, fever, and fatigue. The most widely used chemotherapeutic treatment is ABVD, which contains the drugs doxorubicin (Adriamycin), bleomycin, vinblastine, and dacarbazine.[19]

The other forms of lymphoma are classified as non-Hodgkin's lymphoma (NHL). Many are not truly related to each other, which makes the classification somewhat arbitrary. What they do have in common is that each form is not associated with Reed-Sternberg cells. Treatment for these lymphomas is more complex than it is for Hodgkin's lymphoma and includes combinations of chemotherapy, radiation, monoclonal antibodies, immunotherapy, and bone marrow transplantation. The more slowly developing types are usually treated with fludarabine, cladribine, chlorambucil, and cyclophosphamide. Some forms are best managed with combination therapies. These include CHOP; CVP (cyclophosphamide, vincristine, and prednisone); BACOD (bleomycin, doxorubicin [Adriamycin], cyclophosphamide, vincristine [Oncovin], and dexamethasone); DHAP (dexamethasone, cytarabine, and cisplatin); EPOCH (etoposide, prednisone, vincristine [Oncovin], cyclophosphamide [Neosar] and fluoxymesterone (Halotestin); ESHAP (etoposide, methylprednisolone, cytarabine, and cisplatin); FAD (fludarabine, doxorubicin, and dexamethasone); FMD (fludarabine, mitoxantrone, and dexamethasone); ICE (ifosfamide, carboplatin, and etoposide); MACOP-B (methotrexate, doxorubicin [Adriamycin], cyclophosphamide, vincristine [Oncovin], prednisone, and bleomycin); PMitCEBO (prednisolone, mitoxantrone, cyclophosphamide, etoposide, bleomycin, and vincristine); and Pro-MACE-CytaBOM (prednisone, methotrexate with leucovorin rescue, doxorubicin [Adriamycin], cyclophosphamide [Neosar], etoposide, cytarabine, bleomycin, and vincristine [Oncovin]).[20] The decision of which combination to choose is based on which form of lymphoma is present, the stage it has reached, and the overall condition of the patient.

MELANOMA

The skin contains specialized cells called melanocytes. These cells produce the pigment melanin, which is what makes the skin darker or lighter. Although most melanomas appear in the skin, they may occur in other pigmented tissues such as the eyes and the intestines. The National Cancer Institute estimated that there were almost 69,000 new cases of melanoma in the Untied States in 2009 and some 8,650 deaths.[21] It is often considered the most serious type of skin cancer, particularly because it may spread to other organs in the body and become difficult to treat.

The major causes of melanoma of the skin are excessive exposure to ultraviolet rays, particularly through overexposure to sunlight or tanning beds, certain characteristics of the skin such as numerous or unusual moles; fair skin, red or blond hair, and blue or green eyes; and a family history of melanoma. Melanoma occurs mostly in adults, and most melanomas are found in apparently normal areas of skin.

Melanomas that remain localized are much easier to treat than those that have metastasized. Localized melanomas are removed surgically. Those that have spread to regional lymph nodes are treated by surgical removal of the melanoma along with the lymph nodes. Following this, the patient may receive adjuvant high-dose interferon. Interferons are proteins produced by mammalian cells that stimulate the immune system's responses against pathogens and tumors.

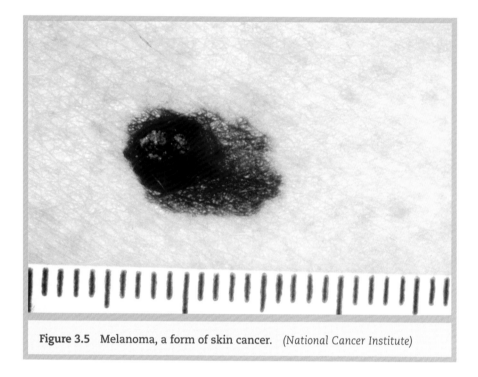

Figure 3.5 Melanoma, a form of skin cancer. *(National Cancer Institute)*

A small number of patients whose melanoma spread to distant sites responded to treatment with interleukin-2 (IL-2). This is not a typical chemotherapeutic drug but rather an immune system stimulator that activates T- and B-lymphocytes to respond to invaders.

Historically, no one regimen of chemotherapy has been shown to be most effective in treating melanoma successfully. Several are available, and the doctor's choice of which to use is based on the patient's condition and the doctor's experience using the various regimens.

MULTIPLE MYELOMA

This is a cancer that begins in plasma cells, the cells of the immune system that produce antibodies. It occurs most often in people age 65 and older and is seen most commonly in African Americans. Patients with this type of cancer tend to suffer with back or bone pain, anemia, bleeding problems, weight loss, and an increase in their susceptibility to infection. In addition, they may suffer from fractures of unexplained origin. The National Cancer Institute estimated that there were more than 20,000 new cases of multiple myeloma in

Treatment Regimens for Melanoma
• Dacarbazine (DTIC), may be used either alone or in combination with other chemotherapy drugs such as carmustine (BCNU) and cisplatin. The combination of these 3 drugs, together with tamoxifen (a hormonal therapy drug), is called the Dartmouth regimen.
• Cisplatin, vinblastine, and DTIC is another chemotherapy combination for treating melanoma. This is known as the CVD regimen.
• Temozolomide (Temodar) is a drug that works similarly to DTIC, but it can be taken orally (a pill). It may be used by itself, although some studies have shown the drug to be more effective when combined with interferon.
• Paclitaxel is a drug sometimes used to treat melanoma, either alone or combined with drugs such as cisplatin or carboplatin.
Source: American Cancer Society. "Detailed Guide: Skin Cancer - Melanoma Chemotherapy." URL: http://www.cancer.org/docroot/CRI/content/CRI_2_4_4X_Chemotherapy_50.asp. Accessed on November 18, 2009.

the United States in 2009 with some 10,000 deaths. The survival rate for multiple myeloma is approximately 50%.

In the very early stages of the disease, treatment is simply a "watch and wait" approach. As long as the patient's condition doesn't worsen too rapidly, it is generally considered better to delay chemotherapy in order to avoid the side effects. As the disease progresses, induction therapy using anticancer drugs will begin. Medications for multiple myeloma include decadron, melophalan, thalidomide, lenalidomide (Revlimid), and bortezomib (Velcade). **Bisphosphonates** are used to prevent fractures.[22] In addition, many patients receive a bone marrow stem cell transplant.

OVARIAN CANCER

The ovaries, the organs responsible for producing the eggs that may someday be fertilized to produce children, are like other organs prone to the development of cancer. If the cancer forms on the surface tissue of the ovary, it is termed an ovarian epithelial carcinoma. If a cancer arises in the egg cells themselves, it is a germ cell tumor. The National Cancer Institute estimated that there were some 21,000 new cases of ovarian cancer and more than 14,000 deaths in the United States in 2009.[23]

Epithelial carcinoma is one of the most common reproductive system malignancies in women. Fifty percent of all cases occur in women older than age 65, and these cancers are the fifth most frequent cause of deaths associated with cancers in women. Unfortunately, there is a definite genetic pattern of inheritance associated with this disease. The risk is very high if a first-degree relative (mother, daughter, sister) has had this type of cancer.

In its early stages ovarian cancer is usually confined to the ovary. As it progresses, the cancer often metastasizes to the lining of the abdominal cavity and to other organs. This, of course, makes the prognosis much less favorable. Treatment is based on which stage of development the cancer has reached.

Most oncologists feel that combination chemotherapy is the best approach to treating ovarian cancer. The drugs are introduced intravenously (into a vein) in cycles, with a rest period between doses. This combination therapy often utilizes a platinum compound such as cisplatin or carboplatin in conjunction with a taxane such as paclitaxel (Taxol) or docetaxel (Taxotere). If the drugs are being given intravenously, carboplatin is often used instead of cisplatin as it has fewer side effects.

In some cases it is felt that direct introduction of the chemotherapy drugs into the abdominal cavity via a catheter is the better method as this will expose the cancer cells in the abdominal lining to the most concentrated dose of the drug.

If, after treatment, the cancer cells return, another course of chemotherapy is warranted. In many cases, the regimen used the first time is repeated. In other situations the oncologist may change the medicines and use topotecan, anthracyclines such as doxorubicin (Adriamycin) and liposomal doxorubicin (Doxil), gemcitabine, cyclophosphamide, vinorelbine (Navelbine), hexamethylmelamine, ifosfamide, and etoposide, among others.[24]

PANCREATIC CANCER

The pancreas is an organ responsible for the production of four hormones, including insulin, which the body uses to control blood sugar levels, and three digestive enzymes. It, too, is another site for the development of cancer. The prognosis for patients with pancreatic cancer is not very promising. The National Cancer Institute estimated that there were some 42,000 new cases of this cancer in the United States in 2009 along with more than 35,000 deaths.[25]

This is a very gloomy prediction indeed. Pancreatic cancer is the fourth leading cause of cancer deaths in the United States.

The response of pancreatic cancer to chemotherapy, surgery, and radiation is poor. Nevertheless, doctors will continue treatment in hope that the therapies will help to prolong the patient's life. Chemotherapy may be used at any stage of pancreatic cancer, but it is often employed in the more advanced stages. It may be used in both neo-adjuvant and adjuvant therapy situations as well.

The most widely used chemotherapeutic drug is gemcitabine (Gemzar). Many oncologists prefer to use 5-fluorouracil (5-FU).[26] In addition to these, oncologists may prescribe other drugs such as cisplatin, irinotecan (Camptosar, or CPT-11), paclitaxel (Taxol), docetaxel (Taxotere), capecitabine (Xeloda), or oxaliplatin (Eloxitan).

PROSTATE CANCER

The prostate gland is responsible for the production of some of the components of semen in men. It is the site of the development of a cancer that occurs usually in older men. The average age of men diagnosed with prostate cancer is 72 years, which means that most men who develop it will die of some other cause of death as they get older. Nevertheless, the National Cancer Institute estimated that there were more than 192,000 new cases of this cancer in the United States in 2009 with more than 27,000 deaths.[27] How this cancer is treated is based on patient age and coexisting medical problems.

Because chemotherapy targets cancer cells that grow quickly, and prostate cancer cells generally grow very slowly, its use to treat this form of cancer is limited and is rarely the first choice of treatment. There are several approaches to treating prostate cancer before chemotherapy is employed. One is brachytherapy, an approach that utilizes the implantation of radioactive "seeds" into the prostate gland itself. The radiation is designed to kill the cancerous cells. Radiation therapy using a thin beam of radiation aimed at the prostate from outside the body is also employed to treat this form of cancer.

Another approach to treatment is cryotherapy. Here, ultra-thin needles are inserted into the gland and extremely cold gases are injected to freeze and destroy cancerous cells. The procedure is minimally invasive and is not associated with serious side effects.

The male hormone testosterone is known to help prostate cancer cells grow. Hormone therapy aimed at reducing testosterone production is used to minimize cancer cell growth. This includes the use of estrogen, a female hormone, and anti-androgen drugs (those that reduce testosterone production).

Surgery to remove the prostate is not an uncommon procedure, especially in the early stages of the disease. In addition, a "watch and wait" approach is often used, especially in the early stages, with older patients, and if it is determined that the cancer is very slow growing.

If the cancer is in an advanced stage and if metastasis has occurred, particularly to the bones, chemotherapy is often used. One of the biggest problems with bone metastases is the associated pain. The chemotherapy is useful in relieving this. The most widely used drugs include mitozantrone, doxorubicin, etoposide, vinblastine, docetaxel, and paclitaxel.

SQUAMOUS CELL CARCINOMA

Another of the nonmelanoma forms of skin cancer is squamous cell carcinoma. Squamous cells are the flat, tile-like cells that form the surface of the skin. As with melanoma, overexposure to sunlight is probably the number one cause of this type of cancer. This form of cancer may also occur in other areas of the body, including the prostate gland, cervix, lips, lungs, urinary bladder, mouth, and esophagus. In some of these areas, human papillomavirus (HPV) has been implicated as the cause.

The risk of metastasis for this form of cancer is very low, but not as low as that of basal cell carcinoma. Nevertheless, if metastasis does occur, treatment must take place. On the skin, mouth, throat, and neck the usual treatment is surgical excision. This may not be a viable option if the cancer occurs in such areas as the eyelids, scalp, nose, and legs. In these cases, cryosurgery is used.

Radiation therapy is used in older patients with extensive cancer in areas that are difficult to treat surgically. It is also used as an adjuvant treatment after surgery if there is a possibility that not all of the cancerous cells were removed.

In advanced cases of squamous cell carcinoma, 13-cis-retinoic acid (derived from vitamin A and also used to treat acne) and interferon-2A have been used as chemotherapeutic drugs. Some studies have shown that they work better in combination. For simple cases of squamous cell carcinoma that remain localized (carcinoma *in situ*), topical fluorouracil (5-FU) has been effective.

4

How Anticancer Drugs Work

Tom had been told that he was suffering from osteosarcoma. He was not surprised since he had been experiencing worsening pain in his arm and a continuous increase in the size of the tumor that had developed in his humerus (the upper arm bone).

The oncologist wanted to avoid amputating the arm, if possible, so that Tom could lead a normal life after the cancer was defeated. He used a combination of neo-adjuvant therapy, surgery, and then adjuvant therapy to save the arm.

As far as the cancer was concerned, this approach seemed to be successful. Tom began his course of chemotherapy about a month prior to the surgery, underwent the procedure, and then continued with his drug treatments after he returned home from the hospital.

Within a few weeks, Tom began to experience nausea and vomiting, hair loss, diarrhea, fatigue, weakness, and loss of appetite. He discussed this with his doctor and found out that these reactions are very common in patients receiving chemotherapy. Tom was not very pleased with this answer. He asked why this was happening and was told that it all had to do with how the medications affected both the cancer cells and the normal cells in his body. The good news was that the symptoms would clear up over time as soon as he was able to stop taking the medications.

HOW CELLS WORK

In order to understand how chemotherapy actually works on cells, it is necessary to understand the basics of how cells normally function. With this understanding, one can see where in the cell, or in the cell cycle, a chemotherapeutic drug goes into action.

THE CELL CYCLE

Almost all cells in the body undergo a cell cycle. This includes the process of mitosis, which is cell division that produces two new, genetically identical daughter cells from a mother cell. Not all cells complete a cell cycle, however. For example, mature red blood cells do not possess a nucleus and, therefore, cannot undergo mitosis. The nucleus is the "controller" when it comes to cell division. Another example of a cell that does not undergo mitosis and, therefore, doesn't complete cell cycles is a mature neuron. In order to mature, these cells did undergo mitosis at an earlier point in their development. They are in what is called the G_0 phase of the cell cycle. This will be discussed below.

After a cell undergoes a mitotic division, it enters into what is termed interphase. This phase of the cycle takes up a lot of time, but will vary in length from cell type to cell type. It consists of several stages that begin with what is termed G_1 (G stands for "gap"). Some cells then enter a phase called G_0—a resting phase during which the cell is in a state of quiescence. In cells that will no longer divide, this is actually a senescent state and they will remain there for the rest of their lives. As mentioned above, neurons, multinucleated muscle cells, and red blood cells are locked into this phase.

In the G_1 stage the cell is growing as well as producing enzymes needed for the synthesis of DNA in the next phase (S phase). The cell's activity rate speeds up to normal during G_1 as it was considerably slowed down during mitosis so that energy could be directed towards cell division. In a human cell that divides every 24 hours, this phase takes approximately 9 hours to complete.

The next stage is the S phase, during which DNA is replicated. This step is necessary because during anaphase of mitosis (discussed below) chromosomes are split into their two component sister chromatids (a chromatid is one arm of a complete chromosome) as each becomes part of the nucleus

The Cell Cycle

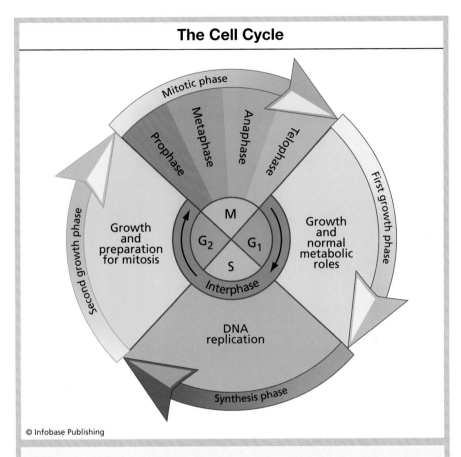

Figure 4.1   This is the cell cycle that most cells undergo. It is divided into several phases and begins with what is termed the G_1 phase that involves cell growth and the production of enzymes necessary for the next phase of the cycle. Many cells enter into the G_0 phase (not shown)—a resting phase—before continuing on with the cycle that leads to another mitotic division, or they remain in this phase for the rest of their lives and never divide again.

of two separate cells. A new matching chromatid must be produced in the daughter cell so that when it matures into a mother cell, division may take place once again.

The last stage is termed G_2. In this stage the cell continues to grow and prepare for the next mitotic division. Many proteins are produced during this stage, as well as microtubules that are necessary for cell division during the upcoming stage of mitosis. This is usually the shortest of the stages in inter-phase. It is generally completed in four to five hours.

MITOSIS

During this stage of the cell cycle, division takes place in the nucleus (karyokinesis) and in the cell itself (cytokinesis). The end result is the production of two daughter cells from one mother cell. Each daughter cell is an exact replica of the mother cell and both contain the same number of chromosomes as the mother. The only difference is that, at this point, the chromosomes are chromatids and contain half the normal amount of DNA. This is why the S phase of interphase is necessary.

The mitotic process occurs in four phases. The first is prophase, during which the loosely bundled chromosomes (chromatin) in the nucleus begin to condense into actual chromosomes. Outside the nucleus, structures known as centrioles migrate to the poles of the cell and begin to generate spindle fibers (a polymerization of the protein tubulin) that will attach to the centromeres on each chromosome. These structures hold the sister chromatids together on each chromosome. At the same time, the nuclear envelope disintegrates so that the spindle fibers can make contact with the centromeres. The chromosomes are now able to migrate to the imaginary equator of the cell, equidistant between the two poles.

The second phase is metaphase, during which the chromosomes are lined up in single file along the equator of the cell (metaphase plate). This alignment is made possible by the fact that the degree of "tug" being applied by the spindle fibers coming from the opposing centrioles is equal.

The third phase is anaphase, during which the sister chromatids are separated from each other due to the recoiling of the spindle fibers. The proteins that bind the sister chromatids together are cleaved, which allows the separation to occur. The cell begins to elongate during this phase and the plasma membrane begins to fold in towards the center. Eventually this will continue to the point where two separate cells are created.

The final phase is telophase, during which the chromatids have separated from each other at such a distance that they are now incorporated into two distinctive cells. The cell itself has continued to elongate, with the plasma

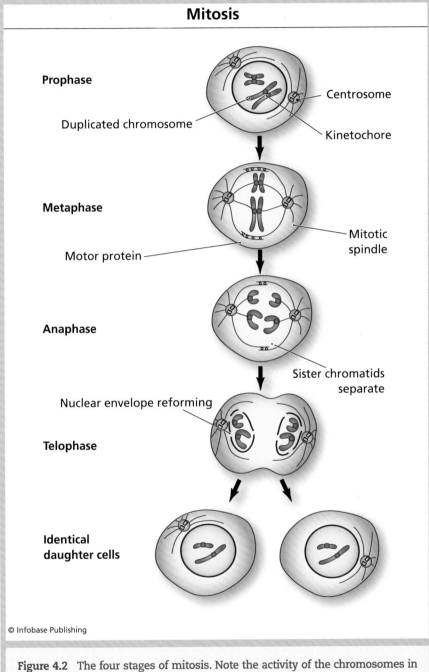

Mitosis

Prophase

Duplicated chromosome

Centrosome

Kinetochore

Metaphase

Motor protein

Mitotic spindle

Anaphase

Sister chromatids separate

Nuclear envelope reforming

Telophase

Identical daughter cells

© Infobase Publishing

Figure 4.2 The four stages of mitosis. Note the activity of the chromosomes in each stage and the eventual creation of two daughter cells.

membrane folding in to actually separate the two cells. A new nuclear envelope develops from fragments of the parent cell's nuclear membrane. The chromatids uncoil once again and go back to the state that they were in during interphase in the mother cell. At this point the cells are still not separated from each other. The mitotic process is complete, but cell division is not.

In order to separate the daughter cells from each other, cytokinesis must occur. This process is not a part of mitosis; it begins during telophase. A cleavage furrow forms from the plasma membrane where the metaphase plate used to be. This achieves complete compartmentalization of the two cells. Several protein and enzyme activities allow the two cells to separate at this juncture.

THE COMPONENTS OF THE CELL

Cells are extremely complex structures that contain numerous organelles, structures that perform specific functions crucial to the survival of the cell. For the most part, each type of cell in the human body possesses virtually all of the same organelles. There are some structures, such as cilia (hairlike structures on the outer surface of some types of cells) that are found in only a few select types of tissue. On the other hand, almost all cells, with the exceptions noted above, have a nucleus or, as in the case of muscle cells, have several nuclei. Table 4.1 summarizes the functions of the organelles found in animal cells.

Because many drugs act directly on the DNA in the cancer cells, it is important to understand its structure as well. Since James Watson, Francis Crick, Maurice Wilkins, and Rosalind Franklin discovered the actual construction of the DNA molecule, scientists have been able to work with it in many ways. This knowledge also helps to develop chemotherapies that will directly affect DNA and, it is hoped, bring about a cure for many cancers.

DNA is referred to as a double helix. Basically, this is like a ladder made of rubber that can be twisted into a spiral. The entire molecule is made up of nucleotides. These represent the rungs of the ladder with their phosphate group backbone being the equivalent of the upright arms of the ladder. In order to hold the two sides together, nitrogenous bases, adenine, guanine (both classified as purines), cytosine, and thymine (both classified as pyrimidines) link up and remain connected due to hydrogen bonding. The only natural combinations are A-T and G-C.

Table 4.1 Cellular Organelles and Their Functions	
Organelle	Function
Nucleus	Isolates and protects chromosomes from cellular chemical activity, directs function of the cell.
Nucleolus	An organelle within the nucleus that produces ribosomes.
Ribosomes	Organelles used for making proteins from amino acids.
Endoplasmic reticulum (ER)	An interconnected network of tubules, cisternae (sac-like structures) and vesicles that exists in three different forms depending on the cell type. *Rough ER (RER)*: The surface is studded with ribosomes (so it looks rough in an electron micrograph). Protein synthesis occurs here. *Smooth ER (SER)*: Used for synthesis of lipids and steroids, drug detoxification, and metabolism of carbohydrates. *Sarcoplasmic Reticulum (SR)*: A specialized smooth ER found in skeletal and smooth muscle cells. It is used to store and pump calcium ions during muscle contraction.
Golgi apparatus	Processes and packages proteins and lipids for transport within or outside of the cell.
Lysosomes	One of the protein (enzyme) packages created by the Golgi apparatus. Used for digestion of food particles, engulfed bacteria and viruses, and excess or worn-out organelles. Also used to digest the cell itself (autolysis) if the cell is dead or damaged beyond repair.
Peroxisomes	These are enzyme packages that bud off from the ER. They contain enzymes that break down toxic peroxides (chemical by-products of certain reactions, such as metabolism of alcohols and fats, within the cell).
Proteasomes	Act as waste disposal units for proteins targeted for destruction.
Mitochondria	Organelles used as the "powerhouses" of the cell. Production of ATP (used for chemical energy by the cell) takes place here.
Centrioles	Barrel-shaped structures that organize spindle fibers used for cell division.
Cilia	In animal cells these are hair-like structures found on the surfaces of some cell types. They function to move mucus upwards in the respiratory system (mucociliary elevators) in order to remove inhaled particles and the mucus itself and they move the ovum away from the ovary towards the uterus in the female reproductive tract.

(continues)

Table 4.1 (continued)	
Organelle	Function
Flagella	Organelles used for locomotion. In animal cells, they are found on sperm, which allows them to "swim" through the female reproductive tract to fertilize an egg.
Cytoplasm	The "fluid" within the cell membrane that contains cytosol (water, salts, and organic molecules), organelles, and inclusions. Most cellular activities occur here.
Cell (plasma) membrane	The structure that surrounds the cell, separating the internal structures from the outside environment. It is semipermeable (selectively permeable) and controls the movement of molecules into and out of the cell.

When a cell is about to divide and DNA must be replicated, the hydrogen bonds break and the double helix "unzips." Each arm of the molecule remains intact to act as a template for the assembly of another arm whose base pairs will link up as before. This creates two strands of DNA that are identical to the original strand. This method of DNA duplication is called semiconservative replication.

MODES OF ACTION

Different anticancer drugs work on different parts of the cell or the cell cycle itself. The numerous side effects experienced by patients using these drugs occur because the chemotherapies are unable to differentiate between healthy cells and cancerous ones. In addition, cells with a rapid metabolic rate, such as the cells of hair follicles, bone marrow, and intestinal lining, are those that are most affected by the drugs.

It is not unusual for an oncologist to treat patients with multiple drugs. This is done because different drugs have different modes of action, so a combination of drugs will target several areas at once, thus giving the patient a better chance at recovering from the cancer. Unfortunately, this also increases the chances of side effects. These vary depending on the drugs being used and the individual patient, as people are known to react differently to the same drug. These will be discussed later in this chapter.

Structure of DNA

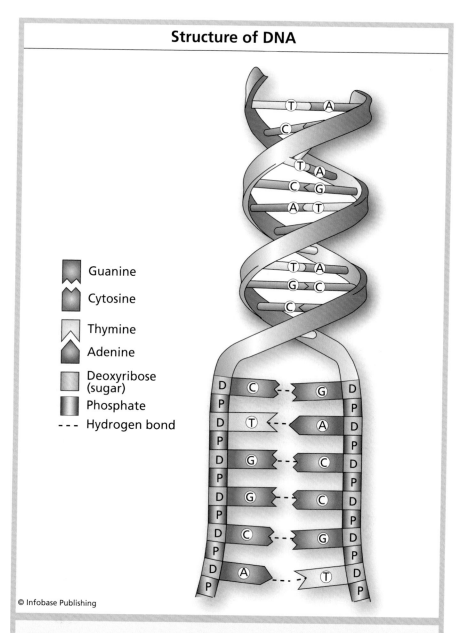

Guanine
Cytosine
Thymine
Adenine
Deoxyribose (sugar)
Phosphate
- - - Hydrogen bond

Figure 4.3 The structure of the DNA molecule. This is a double helix that is held together by nitrogenous bases that attach to each other in a specific fashion as noted. Hydrogen bonding between cytosine and guanine and between adenine and thymine hold the double helix together.

The purpose of chemotherapy is to slow down and, ideally, stop the spread of a cancer. Because normal cells and cancer cells demonstrate few biochemical differences, toxicity becomes a major concern. Large doses of these chemotherapy drugs might kill the cancer cells, but they will most assuredly kill normal cells as well, and possibly kill the patient. This limits the amount of drugs that may be used. In addition, many cancer cells may develop resistance over time to the drugs being used. This is another reason for the multiple drug approach.

The most commonly used drugs share three goals in their approach to treating cancerous cells.[1] The first is to damage the DNA of the cancerous cells. The second is to inhibit the synthesis of new DNA, which will effectively stop the growth of the cancer because the cells will no longer replicate. The third is to stop the mitotic process so no new cells develop from the older ones. If this is successful, the progress of the cancer may be stopped permanently.

There are several classes of drugs that approach the treatment of cancers in different ways.[2] This makes sense as it helps to slow down the cancer cells' ability to become resistant as well as attempting to use every possible means of killing the cells.

ALKYLATING AGENTS

These drugs form new bonds between the strands of DNA molecules. They attach specifically onto the DNA base guanine. This prevents the DNA from dividing, thus limiting the number of cancer cells that will be created. One of the benefits of this form of chemotherapy is that it may be used at any point in the cell cycle, thus making these drugs non-cell-cycle specific. For this reason, these drugs have a high level of effectiveness. Examples are cyclophosphamide, uracil mustard, streptozocin, and busulfan.

ANTHRACYCLINES

This class of drugs is also considered to be antibiotics. They are produced by the fungus *Streptomyces peucetius*. They work to prevent cell division by disrupting the DNA structure, causing it to stop functioning. There are two ways in which this takes place. First, the drugs insert grooves into the base pairs of the DNA, and then they damage the deoxyribose sugar by creating free radicals (ions) that chemically break down the sugars. This category includes

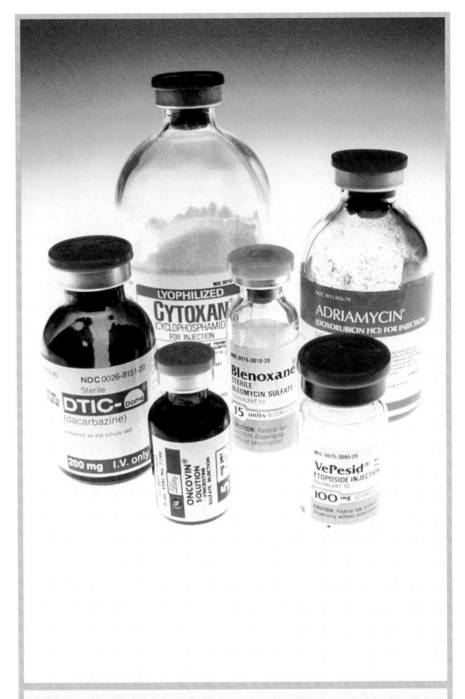

Figure 4.4   Cancer drugs, including two of the more common: cyclophosphamide (Cytoxan) and doxorubicin (Adriamycin).   *(National Cancer Institue)*

daunorubicin (Cerubidine), doxorubicin (Adriamycin), epirubicin (Ellence), and idarubicin (Idamycin).

TOPOISOMERASE INHIBITORS

Enzymes classified as topoisomerases are used to cut the phosphate backbone before DNA is copied. This allows the molecule to unwind. In addition, these enzymes repair breaks after copying. Inhibitors of these enzymes interfere with the repair of the DNA, thus killing the cancer cell because proteins can no longer be made. This leads to apoptosis, or programmed cell death. This class of drugs is cell-cycle specific and can work on a cell only during the S phase of its interphase. Examples of this type of drug include etoposide phosphate (Eposin) and topotecan hydrochloride (Hycamtin).

TUBULIN BINDING AGENTS

As noted in the mitosis discussion above, in order for chromosomes to separate into their individual sister chromatids, spindle fibers are needed. These fibers are made of the globular protein tubulin. Drugs in this group bind to the tubulin and block the formation of the spindles. This causes the mitotic process to stop at metaphase, as the chromatids will no longer be able to separate and the cell will not divide. These drugs are cell-cycle specific and work only during mitosis. Examples of these drugs include vincristine (Oncovin) and vinblastine (Velban).

ANTIMETABOLITES

This class of drugs is designed to interfere with the cancer cell's metabolism in some way that leads to eventual cell death. These medications affect the building up and breaking down of cell components by inhibiting the cell's use of one or more metabolites, chemicals that are part of the cell's normal metabolism. Generally the antimetabolites are similar in chemical structure to the metabolites with which they interfere.

Frequently, antimetabolites will interfere with the production of DNA and RNA because of their chemical similarity to purines and pyrimadines. In addition, some resemble chemicals necessary for metabolism of a vitamin.

An example is methotrexate, which is a folate antagonist. This drug blocks the activity of an enzyme called dihydrofolate reductase, which is necessary for the metabolism of folate (folic acid), a B vitamin (B$_9$) that is used for nucleotide biosynthesis. It is important in the synthesis and repair of DNA. Other antimetabolites include 5-flurouracil (Adrucil), hydroxyurea (Hydrea), gemcitabine (Gemzar), capecitabine (Xeloda), azacitidine (Mylosar), mercaptopurine (Purinethol), thioguanine (Tabloid), fludarabine (Fludara), and cytosine arabinoside (Cytarabine).

MITOTIC INHIBITORS

This class of drugs is derived from natural substances such as plants. Drugs in this category work to interfere with the normal mitotic process by disrupting

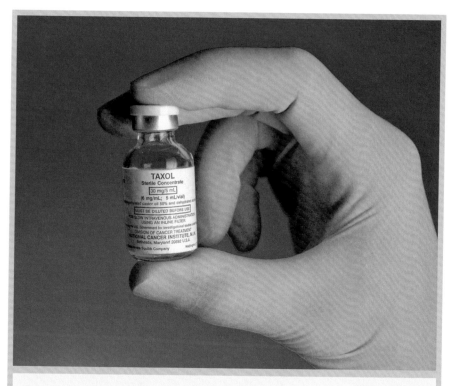

Figure 4.5   Paclitaxel (Taxol), a mitotic inhibitor used in cancer chemotherapy, originally derived from the Pacific yew tree.   (©*Photo Researchers, Inc.*)

microtubule polymerization. This is aimed at stopping cancer cell growth in the M phase of the cell cycle.

These drugs suppress tubulin, a protein that is necessary for mitosis to proceed. This protein is the predominant component of the spindle fibers that are necessary for the separation of the sister chromatids from each other as the cell enters anaphase. When tubulin is disrupted, the cell becomes stuck in metaphase and cannot proceed any further.

Probably the most commonly used mitotic inhibitors include taxanes and *Vinca* alkaloids. Taxanes are derived from the yew tree (genus *Taxus*) and include paclitaxel which is used for lung, ovarian and breast cancer, and doce-taxel which is used for breast, ovarian, and non-small cell lung cancer. Vinca alkaloids are derived from the Madagascar periwinkle and include vinblas-tine, vincristine, vindesine, and vinorelbine which are used to treat leukemias, lymphomas, breast cancer and lung cancer.

IMMUNOSUPPRESSANTS

These drugs act to suppress the immune system in an effort to interfere with the rampant growth of cancerous white blood cells. Medications such as aza-thioprine (Imuran) disrupt rapid cell division and are useful in treating can-cers since these cells divide at an extremely high rate. This drug is also used in patients who have received an organ transplant to slow down the rejection rate by inhibiting white blood cells that attack foreign tissue.

Other immunosuppressive drugs have been used as well, such as dexame-thasone and prednisone, but one of the concerns is that when the immune sys-tem is suppressed, the patient is more susceptible to infections from viruses, fungi, and bacteria. Also, it has been shown that transplant recipients who are using immunosuppressive drugs to reduce the rejection of the transplanted organ tend to have a higher rate of occurrence of various cancers, such as skin cancer, lymphoma, cervical cancer, and liver cancer.[3] This type of treatment is truly a double-edged sword.

SIDE EFFECTS GO ALONG WITH THE TREATMENT

Unfortunately, because anticancer drugs are not able to target only the cancer cells, normal cells are affected and the body responds accordingly. There are several common side effects associated with many cancer medications. Interestingly, some regimens are not associated with serious side effects and may cause none at all.[4] The degree to which a patient experiences side effects will vary depending on the specific drug or drugs used and the individual.

Because cancer chemotherapy is aimed at fast-growing cells and the drugs are distributed throughout the body by the bloodstream, normal cells are also affected. Those most likely to suffer damage from the drugs are cells of the bone marrow, hair follicles, reproductive system, mouth, and digestive tract.[5] In addition, some of the more powerful drugs may damage cells of the nervous system, heart, lungs, kidneys, urinary bladder, and liver.

Nausea and Vomiting

Probably the most common side effects experienced by patients receiving cancer chemotherapy are nausea and vomiting. These symptoms may begin during treatment and last a few hours or, at times, the vomiting may last for a few days. Fortunately, there are several antiemetics (drugs that counteract nausea and vomiting) available with a prescription. The two most commonly prescribed are ondansetron (Zofran) and granisetron (Kytril). They are very effective in quelling the problems. Another is aprepitant (Emend) that is used with other medications to prevent vomiting that may occur within 24 hours of receiving chemotherapy. In addition, it is used with other medications to prevent vomiting that may develop several days after receiving chemotherapy. In addition, many doctors advise their patients to modify their diet, which also helps to keep the situation under control.

Mouth Sores and Changed Taste

Chemotherapeutic damage to the gums and mucous membranes of the mouth and throat can be very painful. In addition, the sores may become infected. Patients also often experience changes in taste due to the sores and irritation to the tongue. The best treatment for these problems is good oral hygiene. Visiting a dentist for a cleaning prior to beginning chemotherapy is always a good idea. In addition, using a mouthwash made of baking soda and water several times each day along with brushing with a soft toothbrush will help to keep the mouth clean and reduce the chances of local infections occurring.

Special mouthwashes may also be used to control pain and bacterial growth. A pharmacist may mix a mouthwash consisting of viscous lidocaine (a topical anesthetic), Maalox (an antacid), and Benadryl (an antihistamine) that may be used to ease the pain and help reduce the occurrence of more mouth sores. To treat fungal infections of the mouth, nystatin mouthwash is also available by prescription.

Changes in taste are not easy to treat. If a patient finds a particular food unpalatable, he or she should keep trying different foods until several are found that are tolerable. It is important to maintain good nutrition through-out life, but this is especially true during periods of chemotherapy. Vitamin supplements and nutritional shakes are often recommended.

Fatigue

Fatigue accompanies treatment with most chemotherapy drugs. It is worse at the beginning and end of a treatment cycle. It tends to linger for an extended period of time and is more pronounced with poor physical fitness and age. Keeping active during periods of fatigue seems to help reduce its effects but, unsurprisingly, excessive exertion is not recommended. In addition, a healthy diet is extremely important in helping to overcome fatigue. In virtually all cases, the fatigue disappears when treatment ends.

Hair Loss

Hair loss is a common side effect of chemotherapy, but not all medications cause it. Since the drugs target rapidly dividing cells and those of the hair fol-licles fall into this category, they are extensively affected by these drugs. Hair loss may occur anywhere on the body where hair is growing, not just on the head. The loss usually occurs after a few treatments, and hair may fall out gradually or in clumps. The remaining hair may become dry and dull. Hair almost always grows back once chemotherapy has stopped. However, it might undergo a change in color or texture.

The key to keeping as much scalp hair as possible is to treat it gently dur-ing chemotherapy. Patients should avoid using dyes, harsh shampoos, and hard brushes. Hair dryers should be used on low heat and the hair should be kept short. When going outside, a hat should be worn to protect hair from sunlight. To reduce friction while sleeping, a satin pillow is recommended.

Peripheral Neuropathy

Damage to nerves may cause numbness or tingling in the extremities. This is known as peripheral neuropathy. It occurs mostly in the fingers and toes. It seems that this side effect is most often associated with vincristine and other tubulin-binding drugs. If these sensations become so debilitating that the patient can no longer use the hands or feet effectively, the dosage of the medication may be reduced or the drug regimen may be changed. The condition disappears after chemotherapy ends.

Anemia, Neutropenia, and Thrombocytopenia

Because chemotherapy destroys some of the bone marrow cells, these three conditions often occur. Anemia is defined as a reduction in the number of red blood cells. This leads to reduced oxygen transport to tissues and is one reason for the fatigue that often accompanies chemotherapy. In addition, weakness, dizziness, pale skin, rapid heart rate, shortness of breath, and feeling cold all may occur to varying degrees. Patients should follow their doctor's instructions for treating fatigue in order to be able to function with anemia. In addition, there is a hormone called erythropoietin that stimulates bone marrow cells to produce more red blood cells. In many cases, patients will benefit from treatment with this hormone.

Neutropenia is a reduction in the number of neutrophils, one of the five types of white blood cells used to fight infections. These are the most abundant of all of the white blood cells and are the first to arrive at the site of an infection. Clearly, a reduction in their numbers will put the patient at a high risk for infections. Other white blood cells may also be reduced. This is known as leucopenia. This reduction in white blood cells may lead to infections, particularly in the mouth, rectum, skin, lungs, and urinary tract.

It is important to avoid situations that might cause infections. This means that hands should be washed often, especially before eating and after going to the bathroom. Avoiding people with respiratory ailments and infections is of extreme importance. This precaution also extends to people who have recently received a vaccine. When shaving, using an electric razor helps to avoid cutting the skin and opening it up to infections.

Thrombocytes (platelets) are disk-like cytoplasmic bodies that circulate in the bloodstream and bring about blood clotting. Their numbers, as well, may be reduced by chemotherapeutic drugs. This will lead to unexpected bleeding, gastrointestinal or urinary tract bleeding, nosebleeds, bleeding gums, headaches, and several other symptoms. Avoiding situations that may lead to cuts and bruises is essential. In addition, if the platelet count becomes too low, a platelet transfusion may be necessary.

Bladder and Kidney Problems

Some chemotherapy drugs are known to irritate or actually damage the kidneys and urinary bladder. Unfortunately, some of the damage may be permanent. In these cases, the urine may change color and appear yellow, orange, or red and may develop a strong medicinal aroma. In addition, the patient may experience painful, burning urination, frequent urination, and even, in some cases, fever and chills. The only possible treatment is to drink plenty of fluids, including water, coffee, tea, soft drinks, and juices, and to eat ice cream, gelatin, and popsicles. This keeps a good flow of urine passing through the system, thus helping to flush it out. Cessation of the medications will allow the symptoms to stop in the absence of permanent damage.

Damage to Skin and Nails

Chemotherapy also affects skin and nails. The skin may develop redness, itching, peeling dryness, and acne, and the nails may become brittle, darkened, and cracked. Cleanliness of the skin is important, along with the use of creams and lotions to keep it moist. Avoidance of perfumes and aftershave lotion is important as these contain alcohol, which has a drying effect on the skin. When the chemotherapy stops, these problems almost always disappear.

5

Treating Cancer Conventionally and Unconventionally

Amanda was a very intelligent and successful professional. She was a top executive at an advertising agency who had earned an MBA with honors from a prestigious university. She kept up with the latest discoveries relating to health and made sure that she kept herself in excellent physical and mental condition so she could lead a long and productive life.

One of the things she made sure to pay attention to was breast self-examination on a routine basis. She knew that this simple activity was an excellent way to help protect women, and even men, from the possible fatal outcome of advanced breast cancer.

One morning, during one of her routine examinations, she discovered a tiny lump in her right breast. It was painless and very small, but she was concerned nonetheless and immediately made an appointment to see her gynecologist so that the doctor could, if necessary, refer Amanda to a health care professional who could treat her. After a mammogram, it was determined that Amanda should see an oncologist.

Amanda was scared. She sat down in the oncologist's office with many questions. The doctor was very sensitive to her needs and fears and explained that there were several treatments available and that she was lucky that the cancer was detected early. The oncologist explained that in addition to the chemotherapies available, there were also some alternative therapies that help the drugs work even better. After her visit, Amanda felt much better about the situation.

Considering that there are so many different types of cancers and that each system of the body is made up of cells that share similarities but also display variations, it is no wonder that the pharmaceutical companies produce an incredible number of anticancer medications. Many years of painstaking research have shown that one type of medication will not treat all varieties of cancer. In fact, because of the genetic and biochemical differences among individuals, a drug that works well on a particular type of cancer in one person may have little or no effect in another.

There are many different approaches to treating patients with cancer. Many include the use of a chemical form of medication; others involve technical approaches such as surgery, lasers, radiation, proton therapy, and several others. The focus here will be on treatment methods that rely on chemicals.

ANGIOGENESIS INHIBITORS

When treating solid tumor cancers, doctors usually choose drugs different from those used to treat leukemias and lymphomas. This is because the cancers will respond differently depending on their origin. For example, one of the newer treatments for solid tumors is the drug bevacizumab (Avastin). This was the first FDA-approved biological therapy for treating solid tumors.[1] Its works by inhibiting the formation of new blood vessels to tumors (**angiogenesis** inhibitors). This approach is of extreme importance as malignant tumors require a large blood supply to nourish the highly metabolically active cells that make up the tumors. Cutting off that supply will "starve" the tumors and lead to a reduction in their size or eliminate them completely.

Solid tumors, in order to establish the constant supply of blood they need to survive, secrete growth factors that stimulate the development of new blood vessels (angiogenesis). One of these factors is a protein known as vascular endothelial growth factor (VEGF). This protein supports tumor growth and promotes formation of new capillaries that surround the tumor. This helps to deliver a rich, nourishing blood supply to the tumor. Bevacizumab is actually an antibody that binds to the VEGF protein in order to inhibit it, thus reducing the tumor's blood supply.

Avastin has been approved for use specifically in treating colorectal cancer (cancer occurring in the descending colon and rectum) that has spread to other sites, some non-small-cell lung cancers (squamous cell carcinoma, large cell carcinoma, and adenocarcinoma) and some breast cancers that have spread to other parts of the body. It is used in conjunction with the anti-cancer drugs 5-FU, leucovorin, and irinotecan or oxaliplatin. This is because the anti-angiogenesis drugs do not perform as well as had been expected and will not cure solid tumor cancers by themselves. In many cases they will only help to prolong the life of the patient without effecting a cure.

A different approach using the same concept was developed when the drugs sunitinib (Sutent) and sorafenib (Nexavar) were created. Unlike bevaci-zumab, these drugs don't target VEGF. Instead, they attach to the receptor sites for VEGF on the endothelial cells of the existing blood vessels, thus blocking the protein's ability to stimulate the cells to proliferate into new blood vessels.[2] Nexavar is designed to be used against kidney cancer, as is Sutent, which is also used to treat gastrointestinal stromal tumors (GIST).

A third approach is seen in conjunction with the drug endostatin (Endo-star), another angiogenesis inhibitor. This drug acts to inhibit endothelial cell proliferation in blood vessels by stimulating apoptosis (programmed cell death). It is also used for non-small-cell lung cancers.

Plasma cells in the bone marrow are responsible for the production of antibodies, chemicals that neutralize antigens, which are foreign proteins that may bring about diseases. For treating multiple myeloma, a cancer of the plasma cells in the bone marrow, the FDA has approved another angiogenesis inhibitor known as bortezomib (Velcade).

Another angiogenesis inhibitor drug, thalidomide, originally prescribed as a tranquilizer, painkiller, and anti-emetic (a drug that inhibits nausea and vomiting), has also been approved to treat multiple myeloma. It is usually given in conjunction with dexamethasone, a corticosteroid. Historically, this drug was responsible for an estimated 20,000 children, mainly in Europe, being born with deformed limbs (phocomelia) when their mothers were given the drug to combat morning sickness during the first trimester of pregnancy.

Thanks to Dr. Frances Oldham Kelsey, a reviewer for the FDA, thalido-mide was never authorized to be marketed in the United States when, in 1960, she insisted that further testing be carried out to determine the drug's safety. During these tests, doctors in Europe, Africa, and Canada realized that using thalidomide during the first trimester caused the limb deformities. American babies were spared from these terrible birth defects.

Much of the research associated with endostatin came from the laboratories of Dr. Judah Folkman at Children's Hospital Boston. Dr. Folkman died in 2008, but the use of endostatin has increased thanks to the work of Dr. Yongzhang Luo, who is also affiliated with Children's Hospital Boston. He discovered a way to refold the active protein, making the production process much cheaper and thus reducing the cost of the medication to patients.

BIOLOGICAL THERAPIES

This form of treatment relies on the body's immune system to attack the cancer or to reduce the side effects associated with the other treatments used. The immune system itself comprises different types of cells and several organs that help to fight off foreign invaders such as bacteria, viruses, fungi, parasites, and any other organisms that may cause diseases to develop. The immune system also protects the body from foreign tissues and must be suppressed to a certain degree when a patient receives an organ transplant from a donor who is not an identical twin.

Some of the main components of the immune system are antibodies, *y*-shaped proteins that bind to antigens (substances that stimulate the production of antibodies) and neutralize them in order to protect the body from damage. Antigens are often proteins that are found on bacterial and viral surfaces, among other places. Their neutralization often protects the body from damage. The immune system will also protect against cancer by possibly recognizing the difference between normal and cancerous cells. It will destroy the cancerous cells as long as this recognition takes place. However, it doesn't always see the cancerous cells as "foreign." In these cases, the cancer may continue to develop.

In instances where the immune system works improperly or is suppressed, cancers may escape detection or destruction and continue to grow and spread. Patients with AIDS or those on immunosuppressive drugs designed to reduce rejection following transplants are at an increased risk for developing cancer for this reason.

Some cells of the immune system produce cytokines, chemicals that allow immune system cells to communicate with each other. Cytotoxic T cells, one form of white blood cell, produce and release proteins that are able to bring about the formation of pores in the cell membranes of foreign, infected, or cancerous cells. This leads to their death due to leakage of fluid from the cytoplasm.

Another method of biological treatment for cancer involves the use of biological response modifiers (BRMs). These chemicals and biological factors, which include interferons, monoclonal antibodies, gene therapy, interleukins, colony-stimulating factors, vaccines, and nonspecific immunomodulating agents, act to change the body's interactions between its immune defenses and cancer cells. These changes include directing, boosting, or restoring the immune system's ability to fight the cancer cells. Many of these may be produced in laboratories in addition to existing naturally.

In general, BRMs may be used to:

- Stop, control, or suppress processes that permit cancer growth.
- Make cancer cells more recognizable and, therefore, more susceptible to destruction by the immune system.
- Boost the killing power of immune system cells, such as T cells, NK cells, and macrophages.
- Alter the growth patterns of cancer cells to promote behavior like that of healthy cells.
- Block or reverse the processes that change a normal cell or a precancerous cell into a cancerous cell.
- Enhance the body's ability to repair or replace normal cells damaged or destroyed by other forms of cancer treatment, such as chemotherapy or radiation.
- Prevent cancer cells from spreading to other parts of the body.[3]

Some of these are used alone or in combination with others as well as being administered in conjunction with radiation therapy and standard chemotherapy. The FDA has approved several BRMs for use in treating specific forms of cancer.

Interferons (IFNs) occur naturally in the body and may be produced in the laboratory. Three forms exist, known as alpha, beta, and gamma. Interferon alpha is the type used most widely to treat cancers. They are cytokines that may improve the manner in which a patient's immune system acts on cancer cells, or they may act directly against cancer cells by helping to direct them into becoming more normal or by slowing their growth. They are approved

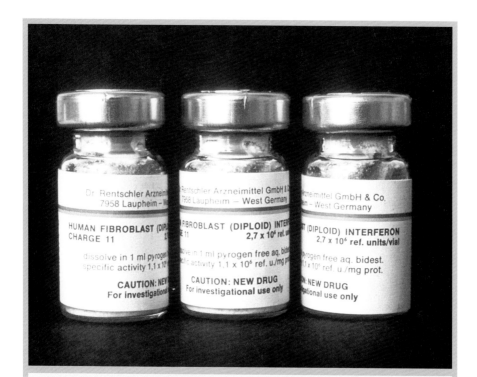

Figure 5.1 Interferons are proteins that occur naturally in the body and may be produced in the laboratory and used as a biological therapy to stimulate the immune system's responses against pathogens and tumors. *(National Cancer Institute)*

for treating Kaposi's sarcoma, a cancer associated with AIDS, chronic myeloid leukemia, melanoma, and hairy cell leukemia. They may also be effective in treating kidney cancer and non-Hodgkin's lymphoma.

Monoclonal antibodies (MOABs or MoABs) are made by a single type of cell and are specific for a single antigen. They are made by injecting mice with human cancer cells. The murine immune system makes antibodies to these cancer cells. Specifically, it is the plasma cells of the murine immune system that make these antibodies, so researchers remove the plasma cells that have now been programmed to make anticancer antibodies and fuse them to laboratory-grown cells to make hybrids known as hybridomas. These cells will continue to make the specific antibodies (MOABs) to the cancer cells.

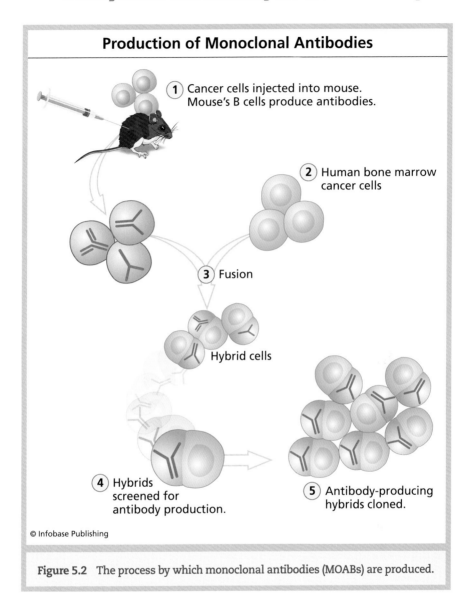

Figure 5.2 The process by which monoclonal antibodies (MOABs) are produced.

MOABs work in several ways to combat cancer. If they have been pro-grammed to act against specific cancer cell growth factors, they will inhibit the growth of the cancerous cells. They might react with specific types of can-cer cells, thus boosting the patient's immune system response to those cancer cells. MOABs may be linked to toxins, radioisotopes, anticancer drugs, or other BRMs. When they find the specific cancer cells they are programmed to detect, they deliver the poisonous substance they are attached to directly to the cell, killing it. They are approved for treating non-Hodgkin's lymphoma and breast cancer in patients with tumors that produce excess amounts of a protein called HER2. Research is under way to determine if MOABs may be used to treat several different forms of cancer as well.

Gene therapy is in the experimental stages. This procedure inserts genes into a patient's cells to enhance their activity. If genes are inserted into an immune system cell, researchers hope that its anticancer activity will greatly improve, thus affording the patient a much more positive prognosis.

Interleukins (ILs) are cytokines that occur naturally and may be produced in the laboratory. Of the many types, interleukin-2 (IL-2) has been studied the most for its cancer-fighting properties. It works to stimulate the growth and activity of immune cells that fight cancers, particularly lymphocytes, one type of white blood cell. These chemicals are approved for treating metastatic melanoma and metastatic kidney cancer. Researchers are continuing to study the possibilities of using ILs to fight several other forms of cancer.

Colony-stimulating factors (CSFs) do not affect cancer cells directly. Rather, they are chemicals that stimulate the bone marrow stem cells into dividing and developing into white blood cells (the cells that make up most of the immune system), platelets for blood clotting, and red blood cells for carrying oxygen to the tissues.

Because many traditional anticancer drugs damage bone marrow, patients are left weak and susceptible to infections after taking these drugs. They may become anemic due to a lowered red blood cell count, bleed more easily due to a reduction in the production of platelets, and develop more infections, colds, and influenza due to a reduced white blood cell count. By stimulating the bone marrow, CSFs help to reverse this clinical picture. So, not only can the patients avoid these problems to some degree, but doctors may give higher doses of the traditional anticancer drugs without being overly concerned that the patients will need blood transfusions.

The most commonly used CSFs are interleukin-11 (oprelveken), G-CSF (filgrastim), GM-CSF (sargramostim), and erythropoietin (epoetin). Interleukin-11 stimulates the bone marrow to produce more platelets so patients avoid the risks of excessive bleeding. G-CSF and GM-CSF stimulate an increased production of white blood cells to help patients fight infections. Erythropoietin is a naturally occurring hormone produced by the kidneys that may also be artificially produced in labs. It stimulates the bone marrow to make more erythrocytes (red blood cells), thus aiding patients in avoiding anemia.

Cancer vaccines, unlike common vaccines that help prevent diseases such as influenza, measles, mumps, and chicken pox before they occur, are designed to either treat existing cancers (therapeutic) or to help the body prevent their occurrence (prophylactic). The latter are designed to target viruses that are known to cause cancers. An example is the Gardasil vaccine, which targets four strains of human papillomavirus (HPV) that are known to be associated with cervical, vulvar, and vaginal cancers as well as genital warts. Another example is the vaccine against hepatitis B virus (HBV), which is associated with liver cancer in chronic cases. Others are still in the experimental stage. The vaccines may eliminate cancer cells left over after conventional treatment, prevent the recurrence of a cancer, or halt the growth of existing tumors.

Nonspecific immunomodulating agents act to indirectly augment the immune system or directly stimulate it. The agents target cells of the immune system leading to production of immunoglobulins (nonspecific antibodies found in the blood plasma and other body fluids) and cytokines. Two of these agents are levamisol and bacillus Calmette-Guerin (BCG).

Levamisol is used in conjunction with the traditional anticancer drug fluorouracil (5-FU) to help restore a depressed immune system when treating stage III colon cancer. BCG, used outside of the United States as a vaccine for tuberculosis, is used to treat superficial bladder cancer after surgery because it stimulates an immune response.

COX-1 AND COX-2 INHIBITORS

The enzymes known as cyclooxygenase 1 and 2 (COX-1 and COX-2) are used by the body to produce prostaglandins, a type of chemical messenger involved in the inflammatory response, contraction of smooth muscles, and control of body temperature. These enzymes are produced in response to inflammation and by cancerous and precancerous tissue. Nonsteroidal anti-inflammatory drugs (NSAIDs) such as aspirin, ibuprofen, naproxen, and celocoxib (Celebrex) are classified as COX-1 and/or COX-2 inhibitors. Thus, they are useful in treating inflammation and fevers.

More than 10 years of research have shown that people who regularly use drugs that block COX enzymes have lower rates of some precancers, cancers, and cancer-related deaths.[4] The studies indicate that the best response is with colorectal cancer, but others have also responded. The inhibition of the COX pathway changes certain traits of the cancer cells. The result is less proliferation, increased apoptosis, angiogenesis inhibition, and an increase in the body's immune response.

ALTERNATIVE APPROACHES

Although thousands of researchers throughout the world have been doing research for thousands of years to develop methods of treating cancer, the work still goes on. The Western medicine methods that scientists hope will lead to medications that eventually receive approval from the FDA or similar agencies in other countries utilize most of the energies spent on this research. Nevertheless, nontraditional approaches have also been studied for thousands of years. Often, however, these studies are not performed in reputable, recognized laboratories associated with hospitals and universities. This is one major reason why the FDA and its counterparts throughout the world usually don't approve the medicines associated with these studies. Some of the most common alternative medicines are discussed here.

AMYGDALIN

Amygdalin is classified as a cyanogenic glucoside. That is, it is a compound that contains sugar and produces cyanide when metabolized by any of several enzymes, including beta-glucosidase, which is present in the human small intestine. It is found in the seeds of several fruits, among them apricots, apples, bitter almonds, and black cherries. It was first isolated in 1830 and used to treat cancer in Russia in 1845 and in the United States in the1920s. However, since cyanide is highly toxic, it was considered to be too dangerous and its use was discontinued. In the 1950s a synthetic form, claimed to be nontoxic, was created in the United States and marketed as a meat preservative. This form was later marketed as laetrile (a shortening of its chemical name laevomandelonitrile) to treat cancer. It was also called vitamin B-17 by Ernst Krebs Jr. in 1956 in an effort to avoid federal legislation concerning the marketing of drugs and to make as much money as possible thanks to the public's extreme interest in vitamins.[5]

In 1972 Benno C. Schmidt Sr., a board member of New York's Memorial Sloan-Kettering Cancer Center, wanted to prove that laetrile was completely ineffective in treating cancer. He was one of many health care professionals who held this opinion, and he felt that with conclusive, properly performed research, the chemical could be officially taken off the market.[6]

A researcher at the hospital, Dr. Kanematsu Sugiura, led the team that conducted the research. Dr. Sugiura's team found that laetrile could inhibit the growth of secondary tumors in mice, but it had no effect on the primary tumors. He repeated his work several times with the same results. This study was uncontrolled. That is, there was no group included that did not receive the drug. All of the mice were given laetrile. Other researchers were unable to repeat his results, but his successes, although far too preliminary to confirm the usefulness of the drug, were leaked to supporters of laetrile and public opinion moved in favor of the use of the drug to treat cancer.

Other researchers at Sloan-Kettering repeated the research, but this time used a control group that received a **placebo** (an inert material that would have no effect). Sugiura performed the pathologic analysis of the mice without knowing which ones actually received the laetrile. This time, the drug showed no more activity than the placebo.[7] In 1974 the American Cancer Society called the use of laetrile quackery, and its use in the United States was never approved by the FDA. However, because the Mexican government did not outlaw the drug, many Americans travel to Mexico for treatment.

714-X (TRIMETHYLAMINOHYDROXYBICYCLO-HEPTANE CHLORIDE)

This drug was developed in Canada. It is naturally derived **camphor** that has been modified to make it safe. The drug is not designed to kill cancer cells directly, but to revitalize the immune system.[8] It acts in several ways. One is to reduce the viscosity of lymphatic fluid. This is the fluid that flows through the lymphatic ducts, the circulatory portion of the immune system that helps to drain fluid between cells, carry fats from the digestive system, and transport lymphocytes, one of the types of white blood cells that help to fight infections.

Another way 714-X works is to bring nitrogen to cancer cells. According to the manufacturer, immature cancer cells require large amounts of nitrogen and, when they reach a certain level of need for this element, they secrete a substance that paralyzes the immune system so they can get nitrogen from healthy cells. Nitrogen is carried by 714-X to the cancer cells so that they don't feel the need to secrete this substance, and the immune system continues to work normally, recognizing and destroying the cancer cells.

Because 714-X contains many trace elements, it supposedly brings these elements to the immune system, which allows the inter- and intracellular communication that was blocked by the clogging of the lymphatic system. It is used in conjunction with chemotherapeutic drugs, but medical personnel recommend that it not be used along with angiogenesis inhibitors because a good blood supply is necessary for 714-X to work properly. The FDA has not approved this drug for use in the United States and has placed an import ban on the product. However, it is available in Canada.

ANTINEOPLASTONS

These drugs are an experimental cancer therapy consisting of a mixture of peptides, amino acid derivatives, and amino acids found in human blood and urine. They were developed by Dr. S. R. Burzynski in the 1980s.[9] The amino acids that he found in the blood were identical to those in the urine, so he used urine as his source since it was much easier to obtain.

Burzynski felt that antineoplastons are part of a surveillance system in the body and that they are capable of acting as "molecular switches" that can direct potential cancer cells to divide in normal channels of differentiation. Carcinogenic (cancer-causing) factors that are capable of misdirecting dividing cells may lead to cancers. The antineoplastons that occur naturally work to reverse this, but, according to Burzynski, those with cancers have an insufficient amount.

Several antineoplastons were discovered, but one, antineoplaston A, appeared to be the most effective. Burzynski further purified this into A1 through A5 and patented them in 1985.[10] Critics have claimed that he has not published any evidence to show that actual research was done to support his claims of anticancer activity of antineoplastons.[11] Currently, several clinical trials are being conducted to determine the efficacy of antineoplastons in treating cancers.

CARTILAGE

Cartilage is a type of connective tissue found throughout the body of mammals, amphibians, reptiles, and fish. There are three different types of cartilage found in the human body. These are fibrocartilage, which is found in discs such as those between the vertebrae; hyaline cartilage, which is found (among other places) at the ends of bones where it makes movement of the joint easier; and elastic cartilage, which is found in the outer ear and the nose.

Cartilage from both sharks and cows (bovine) has been used to treat cancer for more than 30 years. It has not been approved as a cancer treatment by the FDA, but it is marketed as a dietary supplement. This means that neither FDA approval nor a doctor's prescription is needed for its sale. Supposedly, cartilage displays three different forms of antitumor potential. It may stimulate the immune system, kill cancer cells directly, and act as an angiogenesis inhibitor. Two of the latter have been identified in bovine cartilage and one in shark cartilage. To date, more than a half-dozen clinical studies have been performed to determine the efficacy of shark cartilage in treating cancer. Because cartilage has no blood supply, it was hypothesized that there must be an angiogenesis inhibitor in the cartilage itself. Much research has been done to determine if this is, indeed, the case.[12] No conclusive results, however, have been found.

Cartilage is made of the protein collagen as well as glycosaminoglycans (polysaccharides). The major glycosaminoglycan is chondroitin sulfate, which is sold as a dietary supplement designed to aid in the treatment of arthritis because it is touted as helping to sustain joint cartilage integrity. Research has not shown that glycosaminoglycans have the ability to act as angiogenesis inhibitors. However, evidence exists showing that shark cartilage contains at least one angiogenesis inhibitor with a glycosaminoglycan constituent. Nevertheless, the FDA has not approved the use of shark cartilage as a treatment for cancer. Also, because of the widespread interest in shark cartilage for treating cancer, sales have been increasing and the number of sharks in the world's oceans has been decreasing.

COENZYME Q_{10} (UBIQUINONE)

Coenzyme Q is synthesized naturally in several forms in humans and many mammals. Q_{10} is the predominant form in humans and has been the one most often used to aid in cancer treatment. It helps cells produce energy through aerobic respiration and it acts as an **antioxidant**. Antioxidants neutralize free radicals, ions that form due to several different causes, including toxins, radiation, pollution, and several others. Once tissues are exposed to these ions, damage may occur, particularly to DNA and lipids. In addition to being an antioxidant, coenzyme Q_{10} also protects the heart from damage caused by chemotherapy and acts as an immune system stimulant.

Coenzyme Q_{10} is found throughout the body, but is most highly concentrated in the pancreas, liver, heart, and kidneys. Studies have shown that it is able to protect the heart from damage caused by the administration of anthracycline anticancer drugs such as doxorubicin. Other research has shown that it does stimulate the immune system, thus indirectly fighting cancer. Because of this fact, coenzyme Q_{10} has been used as an adjuvant therapy in patients receiving traditional chemotherapies for various forms of cancer.[13]

Other research has shown that analogues (chemicals similar to the original, but not identical to it) of coenzyme Q_{10} may have a direct effect on cancer cells. The research showed that these analogues were capable of inhibiting the growth of cancer cells transplanted into mice and rats and blocking the proliferation of cancer cells in experiments performed *in vitro*.[14] This led to the suggestion that the analogues acted as antimetabolites, drugs that are similar to the naturally occurring chemicals required for a normal reaction to take place within a cell, but different enough to interfere with that reaction.

AROMATHERAPY AND ESSENTIAL OILS

Aromatherapy involves the use of essential oils (volatile oils) derived from plant sources aimed at improving an individual's spiritual, physical, and emotional health. Cancer patients have used this form of therapy mainly as a supportive tool to help their bodies cope with the disease and the treatment. It may be used in conjunction with palliative therapies such as acupuncture and massage and with traditional chemotherapy, surgery, and radiation therapy. The oils must be naturally extracted from plant sources. Any oils that have been produced via chemical solvents are not classified as true essential oils.

The oils are administered topically or by inhalation and are generally diluted before use. Their mode of action is suggested to be the result of odorant molecules from the oils having a direct effect on the limbic system, the brain's center of emotions and behavior. In addition, when the oils are applied topically, they may possess analgesic, anti-inflammatory, and anesthetic properties.

Research using animals has shown both sedative and stimulatory effects in addition to positive effects on the immune system and behavior. Additional studies in humans using functional imaging techniques have demonstrated that essential oils have an effect on reaction time, task performance, and certain autonomic (involuntary) responses.[15] Accepted, controlled studies showing cures for different forms of cancer are not found in the medical literature. Several studies have been performed that show the beneficial effects of aromatherapy in treating various side effects of chemotherapy and cancer-related depression, anxiety, and stress.[16]

ESSIAC/FLOR·ESSENCE

Essiac was developed in Canada in the 1920s by Rene M. Caisse, a nurse from Ontario. The product's name is her last name spelled backward. She got the formula from a woman who claimed to have had breast cancer that was cured by the compound. The woman said she had gotten the formula from an Ontario Ojibwa medicine man.

These two products are herbal tea mixtures that are intended to detoxify the body and strengthen the immune system.[17] Those who support the use of Essiac also claim that it improves the overall quality of life, relieves pain, lengthens survival time in cancer patients, and may reduce tumor size.

The ingredients included in both teas are burdock root (*Arctium lappa* L.), sheep sorrel (*Rumex acetosella* L.), Indian rhubarb root (*Rheum palmatum* L.), and the inner bark of slippery elm (*Ulmus fulva*). In addition to these ingredients, Flor·Essence also contains watercress (*Nasturtium officinale*), kelp (*Laminaria digitata*), blessed thistle (*Cnicus benedictus* L.), and red clover (*Trifolium pratense* L.).

Individually, the herbs in these compounds have been shown to possess some anticancer, antioxidant, immunostimulatory, and anti-inflammatory properties.[18] In fact, one research study demonstrated that Essiac was able to inhibit prostate cancer cell proliferation.[19] Once again, however, no controlled studies have been performed to support the claims made by the manufacturers of these products. Because these products are marketed as dietary supplements, FDA approval is not needed to sell them.

In the mid-1970s the developer of Essiac submitted both dried and liquid samples to Memorial Sloan-Kettering Cancer Center (MSKCC) in New York and asked that they be tested for anticancer properties. Eight different studies carried out at the medical center on mouse sarcoma tumors were not able to show any anticancer activity. In the early 1980s another sample was submitted to MSKCC and 17 trials were conducted using animal leukemia and tumor models. There was no success in these experiments either.

Animal studies conducted with Flor·Essence also met with no success. In fact, one study showed that the product enhanced tumor growth in vitro.[20] In another research study, both products were shown to stimulate the growth of human breast cancer cells.[21] One more study demonstrated differentiation-inducing and antiproliferative properties only *in vitro* and only at high concentrations.[22] Interestingly, several studies conducted on the individual components of the two teas have actually shown that they do posses antioxidant, anti-inflammatory, and anticancer qualities to some degree.[23]

The product manufacturers have stated that both products may be used while a patient is undergoing chemotherapy or radiation therapy for cancer. However, some proponents of these teas feel that chemotherapy and radiation therapy, because they often interfere with normal immune functions, should be discontinued while the patient is using the teas so that they may reach their maximum level of benefit.

6
Anticancer Drugs and the Economy

Melanie Shouse died at her home in Overland, Missouri, on January 30, 2010, from stage four breast cancer. In 2005 she had been diagnosed with terminal breast cancer. She battled the cancer for four and a half years, receiving chemotherapy. Because of the high cost of health care insurance, she was able to afford only a less expensive catastrophic health plan that required approximately $8,000 of co-payments and deductibles before it would start paying for her treatment. This caused her to put off getting examinations, screening, and treatment. These delays allowed the cancer to progress.

As she started the third round of chemotherapy, her insurance company notified her that it would no longer cover the cost of the medication. At this point Medicare and Medicaid began paying for half the cost of the treatments, but only after she was declared totally disabled. This meant more out-of-pocket expenses.[1]

Melanie's true story is not an uncommon one in today's health care insurance world. Medical and pharmaceutical costs are alarmingly high, health insurance premiums are very expensive, and the insurance companies are quick to deny claims in a substantial number of cases. This problem also presents itself with other forms of cancer therapy.

In April 2009 Shelley Andrews-Buta was preparing for surgery to treat breast cancer that had metastasized to 15 separate sites in her brain. The doctors at the University of California, San Francisco (UCSF) Medical Center had determined that the best course of treatment for the numerous sites of the cancer would be a noninvasive surgical technique known as the "gamma knife." This procedure is able to target a tumor from several different angles without actually cutting into tissues. The tumors may shrink or even be killed without damage to the surrounding healthy brain tissue.

The doctors at the medical center felt confident that this treatment would be very effective in helping Andrews-Buta to recover. The problem was that she needed immediate treatment as she had deteriorated to the point where she was no longer able to walk. Unfortunately, her insurance company was unwilling to pay for the gamma knife surgery to more than five tumors. Instead, they were willing to pay for whole-brain radiation. The company's opinion was that the gamma knife surgery would not improve Andrews-Buta's prognosis any better than whole brain radiation, even though the radiation treatment would most assuredly damage normal brain tissue as well.

The doctors at UCSF disagreed. They stated that their experience with gamma knife surgery was very encouraging and that Andrews-Buta would surely suffer permanent, irreversible changes in her brain with whole-brain radiation. Some of the lasting effects, the doctors said, would be difficulty remembering and speech problems, both of which might become permanent.

As it turned out, there were other insurance companies that would pay for treatment to the 15 sites, so coverage for this form of therapy was not unheard of. Nevertheless, this didn't change the policy of Andrews-Buta's insurance company. Her friends raised more than $30,000 to help cover the cost of treatment. In addition, they held a fund-raiser in June 2009 to pay for the $12,000 she still owed after the treatment was finished.[2]

WHY ARE THE COSTS SO HIGH?

At the end of 2009, a new anticancer drug was approved that will cost $30,000 a month. The drug, Folotyn (pralatrexate), is designed to treat relapsed or refractory peripheral T-cell lymphomas, a group of aggressive neoplasms that accounts for less than 15% of all non-Hodgkin's lymphomas. This form of cancer strikes approximately 5,600 Americans each year.[3] The cost of Folotyn has been criticized as being far too expensive for the benefits derived from its use by patients.

Folotyn costs three times as much as another anticancer drug, Erbitux (cetuximab), that is used to treat colon cancer. Erbitux costs $10,000 a month. Avastin (see Chapter 5), used to treat lung cancer, costs about $8,800 a month.

Drug manufacturers have been raising the prices of drugs in anticipation of the enactment of the recently passed health care reform bill. The bill includes price curbs and many restrictions on the costs of drugs in an effort to help those individuals who cannot afford expensive medications. Pharmaceutical lobbyists won new federal policies they coveted and set a trajectory for long-term industry growth.

The overall cost of drug treatment for cancer also depends on the length of time needed to get the maximum medical benefit. The manufacturer of Folotyn feels that because the drug is used for only a few months, it is no more expensive than some cheaper drugs that are used for a longer period of time. For example, Clolar (clofarabine), which is used to treat acute lymphoblastic leukemia (ALL) in children, costs $34,000 per week, but is used for only 2 weeks. Campath (alemtuzumab) which is used to treat chronic lymphocytic leukemia (CLL), costs $5,000 per week with a treatment regimen lasting 12 weeks. Another drug used to treat CLL is Arzerra (ofatumumab). This drug costs about $98,000 for a 6-month course.

So why do drug manufacturers feel that it is necessary to charge such incredibly high prices for some of their medications? Estimates of the cost of developing a new drug range from $800 million to approximately $2 billion per drug.[4] These costs are sure to rise as more and more intense and expensive research is carried out to develop more efficacious drugs for more and more conditions.

Why are these development costs so high? In the United States as well as in other nations, funding for pharmaceutical research comes mainly from private industry. The research being funded is usually based on prior publicly funded research studies carried out at universities and hospitals. Scientists attempting to come up with a new drug will frequently look at 5,000 to 10,000 new chemical inventions that appear to have promise. From this enormous pool of possibilities, they will narrow down the field to approximately 250 compounds that will be tested in preclinical and animal studies. From this much reduced group of candidates, only about 10 will be considered worthy of qualifying for Phase I human testing to establish clinical safety. The trials usually include only a small number of healthy individuals who will be tested to determine the safety and efficacy of the new compounds.

Any drug that successfully makes it through a Phase I trial will enter a Phase II trial that includes a small group of humans who have the specific condition that the drug is aimed at treating. If the drug appears promising, it will enter a Phase III trial.

Phase III trials are very large and include wide-scale tests on thousands of patients with a certain condition. These studies are controlled: some of the patients receive the drug and others merely get a placebo.

On the average, although 5,000 to 10,000 chemicals are considered at the beginning of the research, the U.S. government usually only grants a license for one product. This happens after 12 to 15 years of research studies. During this time patents are granted, but more years go by before final approval for marketing. Patents are usually valid for 20 years, but after a patent is granted, it still takes several years to get the drug approved. This means that there is less time left on the patent before another company can produce a generic

The First Clinical Trial

Amazingly, clinical trials first began in A.D. 1025 when Avicenna (Abdallah Ibn Sina) wrote *The Canon of Medicine*.[5] In his book Avicenna established a set of rules and regulations to govern clinical testing so that the results would be reliable. Modern clinical trials are still based on these concepts. Avicenna stated:

1. The drug must be free from any extraneous accidental quality.

2. It must be used on a simple, not a composite, disease.

3. The drug must be tested with two contrary types of diseases, because sometimes a drug cures one disease by its essential qualities and another by its accidental ones.

4. The quality of the drug must correspond to the strength of the disease. For example, there are some drugs whose heat is less than the coldness of certain diseases, so that they would have no effect on them.

5. The time of action must be observed, so that essence and accident are not confused.

6. The effect of the drug must be seen to occur constantly or in many cases, for if this did not happen, it was an accidental effect.

7. The experimentation must be done with the human body, for testing a drug on a lion or a horse might not prove anything about its effect on man.

version of the drug. All along, the pharmaceutical companies have to pay out direct costs for drug development and returns on the capital invested on behalf of shareholders. The longer it takes to get approval for the drug, the greater the expenses.

Even with the high costs associated with the sale of drugs, it has been estimated by economists that only about 30% of new medicines actually make enough money during the time they are protected by the patent to cover the costs of development. Drug manufacturers rely heavily on investors. Investors have to be convinced that the drugs the company is testing will be successful and bring in large returns on their investments. Strong patent protection helps this to occur. In order to create successful drugs, the scientists must therefore be creative and insightful while being funded by investors. The investors must be convinced that the scientists are creative and insightful so that they invest.

HOW MUCH SHOULD BE SPENT?

The question of where to draw the line on spending for cancer treatment has been discussed in numerous publications and in interviews on television and radio. Dr. Tito Fojo of the Medical Oncology Branch, Center of Cancer Research at the National Cancer Institute, and Dr. Christine Grady of the Department of Bioethics, the Clinical Center at the National Institutes of Health, addressed this issue in 2009 in a journal article.[6] In regard to the anticancer drug cetuximab, their question was, "Is an additional 1.7 months [the additional overall survival for colorectal cancer patients treated with cetuximab] a benefit regardless of costs and side effects?"

Cetuximab is mainly used to treat non-small-cell carcinoma of the lung. According to Fojo and Grady, 18 weeks of treatment for the lung cancer costs approximately $80,000 and will extend life by an average of 1.2 months. This means that it costs $800,000 to extend a patient's life by one year. When one takes into account the number of patients in the United States that are being treated with this drug, the total cost is about $440 billion per year to extend the lives of 550,000 Americans for just one year. It was suggested that the results of treatment with these drugs be studied to establish a list that shows which ones will extend life by only two months or less. Once this is done, a limit of a $20,000 expenditure could be set.

The problem, of course, is also one of ethics. Nobody can put a price tag on an individual's life. However, according to Fojo and Grady, "The current situation cannot continue. We cannot ignore the cumulative costs of the tests and treatments we recommend and prescribe. As the agents of change, professional societies, including their academic and practicing oncologist members, must lead the way. The time to start is now."

Fojo and Grady made a very logical suggestion based on the controlled expenditures in place in Great Britain. In the United Kingdom, the National Institute for Clinical Excellence (NICE) has set the maximum allowable expenditure for drug treatment at £30,000 (about $55,000) per quality-adjusted life-year (QALY).[7] This maximum is based on the performance record of the different medications. That is, the more effective a medication is at treating a condition, the higher the maximum allowable expenditure.

Fojo and Grady recommended that the maximum allowable expenditure for anticancer drugs in the United States should be set at $129,000. This is the equivalent of the cost of a QALY in a patient on renal dialysis, the treatment used to cleanse the blood when the kidneys no longer do the job.

In the United Kingdom, the maximum allowable expenditure is not always fixed. Drug companies adjust their prices to satisfy the threshold requirements. NICE will assess the drug at the manufacturer's original price. If the drug is rejected, the manufacturer may go back to the National Health Service (one division of which is responsible for new drug approval, similar to the U.S. FDA) and come to an agreement to establish a workable solution. This occurs because, unlike in the United States, in the United Kingdom cost is a factor in the approval process for a drug.

HOW FAR-REACHING ARE THESE HIGH COSTS?

With the increasing costs of cancer chemotherapy, the decision regarding which drug is best to treat the patient relies not only on the doctor's experience and research information but also on the cost to the patient.

Dr. Neal J. Meropol, director of the gastrointestinal cancer and gastrointestinal tumor risk assessment programs at Fox Chase Cancer Center in Philadelphia, Pennsylvania, has stated,

Cancer care is one of the most expensive areas of health care today, and the cost of that care is increasing steadily, for patients and for society as a whole. As physicians, we have a responsibility to understand the impact that the increasing cost of cancer care has on everyone involved. In particular, we need to be able to discuss with our patients the impact that high out-of-pocket expenses might have on them and their families, however difficult that conversation might be. More and more, cost considerations have an appropriate role in the assessment of treatment options.[8]

Meropol feels that not only are the patients affected by the high costs but employers are finding it increasingly difficult to subsidize their employees' health care insurance and the insurance companies are having a much harder time balancing their premiums against their expenditures for medical costs. In addition, doctors are being pressured into providing the "proper" advice to their patients on which drugs to use, and the pharmaceutical companies must cover research and development costs, make a profit, and convince the insurance companies to pay for the treatments.

In light of the extensive number of cancer cases worldwide, the high costs of many anticancer medications are causing a host of problems for society. Patients in lower socio-economic groups might not get the best anticancer drug treatments. Some of the smaller pharmaceutical companies could be forced out of business because of the expenses incurred by the research and development of new anticancer drugs. Taxation of the people would need to increase in order to support public health care programs as these programs attempt to pay for the high cost of medications. As Meropol points out, "Rising costs may be a key impediment to reaching our societal goal of providing high quality cancer care to all citizens."

On a more individual level, many doctors are writing prescriptions for the most modern anticancer drugs, but a large number of patients are not filling those prescriptions. This trend is getting worse, according to Marilyn Stebbens, the pharmacy utilization director for Mercy Medical Group at the CHW Medical Foundation in Sacramento, California.[9] Her job is to work with uninsured and underinsured patients to find programs that help to cover unaffordable medications. Stebbens claimed, "Over the past three years, our referrals from oncology have increased dramatically due to the high cost of many of these drugs." With pharmacy costs often exceeding $50,000, many of these patients will not even begin treatment until they speak with Stebbens and find a program that will help defray these costs.

Stebbens helps patients who have no insurance and very little money and also those who have insurance. The latter group includes the elderly who are covered by Medicare insurance. This insurance has a very limited scope of coverage with low monetary allowances for most drugs and therapies. Those covered by Medicare are often relying on Social Security as their sole source of income and don't have the necessary funds to cover expensive therapies. Stebbens points out, "These are fixed-income individuals. Even if they receive what they consider to be a reasonable Social Security check, a single drug might still cost them as much as $800 per month."

The anticancer drug therapy is not the only cost that must be covered. For example, in light of the fact that most anticancer drugs are associated with several side effects that act upon different systems of the body, expenses rise when these side effects are addressed. An example used by Stebbens is Tarceva, a targeted drug that costs $3,900 per month. It often causes anemia, which requires treatment with Epogen, a drug that costs an additional $550 per month. If an excessive amount of white blood cells are lost, treatment with Neupogen is needed at a further cost of $2,600 for 5 days of therapy. With this sort of clinical picture, a Medicare-insured individual would still have very large out-of-pocket expenses to cover the cost of the drugs.

A conference called "Science of Health Care Disparities" held in February 2009 by the American Association for Cancer Research included a study that showed that an estimated one million Americans go without recommended cancer treatment. Of all cancer patients, Hispanic and African-American patients make up the majority of those who do not receive proper treatment. "A cancer diagnosis can threaten anyone with bankruptcy and financial ruin, no matter what your earning power is," said Peggy McGuire, executive director of the Women's Cancer Resource Center in Oakland, California. "There are many paths you take, but they lead to the same destination: loss of all resources."[10]

In mid-2010, 32 states have legislation pending that involves funding either for payment to patients by insurance companies for expenses relating to clinical trials, funding for cancer research, increased insurance coverage to cover early detection programs, increased taxation on tobacco products whereby the money will be used to fund cancer screening programs, and several other important areas in the prevention and detection of cancer.[11] Unfortunately, none of these is aimed at helping patients pay for expensive cancer chemotherapies. However, in July 2009, the California Assembly Health

Committee voted 10-3 in favor of SB 161, a bill that requires California health insurers to provide equal coverage for oral and intravenous chemotherapy treatments.[12] The reason for this bill was that up to that point, the insurance companies considered the oral form of chemotherapy a pharmaceutical expense whereas the intravenous form was considered a medical expense. Since policies provide better coverage for medical expenses than for pharmaceutical expenses (some don't cover drugs at all), putting this bill into law would provide for coverage regardless of which form of chemotherapy is used by a patient. The bill also passed in the California Senate. Critics of the bill claim that those who pay for their own insurance premiums would be footing the bill for expanded coverage as the costs to insurance companies would increase substantially. The bill was vetoed by Governor Arnold Schwarzenegger on October 11, 2009.

A national survey of cancer patients and their families was completed in 2006 by the Kaiser Family Foundation, *USA Today*, and the Harvard School of Public Health. Twenty-five percent of patients who had health insurance plans reported that they used up all or most of their savings relating to cancer treatments. In this same group, 33% had a problem paying their cancer bills. In addition, 27% of those who had no insurance reported that they or a family member either postponed or simply did not get cancer care because of the expense.[13]

According to the American Society of Clinical Oncologists, the United States spends approximately 16% of its gross domestic product on health care. This amounts to more than $2 trillion. The growth rate of health care spending exceeds that of the overall economy, so that the percentage of the U.S. economy dedicated to health care is expected to reach 20% by 2017. Of this, cancer care expenditures are approximately 5%. However, they are projected to rise. The National Institutes of Health estimates that in 2007 $89 billion was spent on cancer care. This translates to $219.2 billion when indirect costs associated with lost productivity and death are added. Anticancer drugs are now number one in hospital drug expenditures.[14]

Another aspect of the economic impact associated with a diagnosis of cancer relates to employment. It is not unusual for a cancer patient, or one or more members of his or her family, to find it necessary to change jobs, work fewer hours, or even lose jobs because of the disease. In one national survey 19% reported that they fit one or more of these criteria because of cancer in the family. More than one-third were unable to perform their jobs as well and 22% had lower income.[15]

It must also be remembered that economic concerns of the patients and their families have a strong impact on their psychosocial well-being. This may lead to problems in different areas, including employment, social relationships, and the patient's ability to discuss viable treatment plans with the doctor. Many patients feel uncomfortable discussing with their doctors an inability or serious difficulty in paying for drug treatments which, in turn, may very well lead to putting off or totally avoiding treatment.

In the United States, approximately 54% of the moneys paid out to cover health care costs comes from out-of-pocket payments and health insurance. Medicare covers approximately 42% of these costs, which means that tax dollars are helping to pay for a portion of anticancer drug therapy.[16]

In order to cope with the incredible amount of money that is paid out each year, the health insurance carriers, in an effort to remain solvent, have begun to modify their policies in several ways. Many policies require an increase in the patient's responsibility for payment, such as high deductibles, large copayments and increased coinsurance costs. Patients also often have to get referrals and prior authorizations before additional treatments are allowed. Some employers are limiting raises or reducing salaries in order to cover the increases in health insurance premiums.

It is quite clear that the economic impact relating to the extensive usage and high cost of anticancer drugs has far-reaching effects in many areas of the economy. This is a problem that will only continue to get worse unless some major overhauls in the health care system take place.

7

The Future of Anticancer Drug Development

Dr. David Franklin, a cancer research specialist, was busy working in his laboratory one afternoon when the phone rang. He answered it only to hear his mother, Jennifer, on the other end of the call sounding terribly upset and very worried.

"What's the matter, Mom?" he asked her. "Is everything all right?" She told him that she had just received a phone call from her doctor to let her know that she was suffering from Stage I squamous cell carcinoma of the larynx. Unfortunately, many years of smoking cigarettes had taken its toll, and now she was scared.

David had to collect his thoughts. He was shocked and terribly distressed by the news. He talked to his mother for quite some time in an effort to calm her down and get as much information as he could. He promised her he would call her doctor to discuss the case.

The ironic part about the situation, and perhaps the most encouraging one, was that David had been doing research on the development of a new anticancer drug specifically designed to treat squamous cell carcinomas. Clinical trials were about to begin and he was heartened by the fact that his preliminary results were very successful. His mother's condition gave him new incentive to redouble his efforts to get his drug on the market.

HOW DOES A NEW MEDICATION GET APPROVAL?

Because of what was happening to his mother, David became more zealous in his efforts to get approval for his new anticancer drug. He knew that when all of his clinical trials were done, he could submit an application to the Food and Drug Administration (FDA) to approve its marketing. The FDA, a branch of the U.S. Department of Health and Human Services, is responsible for approving the sale of new medications, medical and radiological devices, food and cosmetics, biologics, and veterinary drugs.

More specifically, the Center for Drug Evaluation and Research (CDER) is the branch of the FDA that ensures that a drug is safe and effective.[1] It doesn't test each drug, but CDER's Office of Testing and Research conducts limited research in the areas of drug quality, safety, and effectiveness. It is the largest of the FDA's five divisions and is responsible for both prescription and over-the-counter medications.

When a pharmaceutical company wants to get a new drug approved, it must perform rigorous tests and prove that it is safe and effective. The company must file an investigational new drug (IND) application to CDER. This is done after preliminary research in the laboratory yields promising results. The application is reviewed by CDER's chemists, statisticians, physicians, pharmacologists, and various other scientists. The application must contain information on animal pharmacology and toxicology studies, manufacturing information, and clinical protocols and investigator information.

When the IND is approved, clinical trials may begin. Clinical trials use human subjects to determine safety, efficacy, and what side effects might occur. Strict regulations and guidelines must be adhered to during this phase of testing. Once the manufacturer is satisfied that there is enough evidence about the drug's safety and effectiveness to meet FDA guidelines, a new drug application (NDA) is submitted, which includes full information on manufacturing specifications, method of analysis of each dosage form that is intended to be marketed, manufacturing specifications, packaging and labeling for both consumers and physicians, and the results of any new toxicological studies that have been performed since the IND application was submitted. If everything submitted is satisfactory to the CDER panel, the drug will be approved for marketing.

The process of performing clinical trials is a long one. The purpose is to determine efficacy and safety of the drug being tested. In order to obtain valid results that the FDA will accept, several phases of trials must be carried out. The drug manufacturer or research laboratory will recruit either healthy volunteers or patients with the condition that the drug is designed to treat.

Since these studies are very expensive, the initial pilot studies are composed of small groups of participants. After these studies are done, larger clinical trials are carried out.

The clinical trials are carried out in phases once the preliminary laboratory studies with animals are completed. A phase 0 study begins the process as an exploratory first-in-human trial. These trials are microdosing studies, in which the dosages used are too little to bring about a therapeutic effect. The purpose is merely to determine if the drug being tested will behave in humans the way it is expected to. Animal studies alone may be inconsistent and the phase 0 study helps to standardize results.

The next step is a phase I clinical trial, in which a small group of healthy subjects is given the drug to determine its safety, efficacy, and tolerability. These studies are often carried out in an inpatient clinic where subjects are observed. The participants receive a dose of the drug that is only a fraction of the dose that would be harmful. Usually, the subjects are healthy, but sometimes they will actually have the disease that the drug is designed to treat.

Phase II clinical trials begin once the safety of the drug has been confirmed by phase I studies. These trials may be divided into IIA and IIB studies where the former is designed to determine dosing requirements and the latter is used to establish efficacy of the drug. It is in this phase that a drug might fail when it is discovered that it is more toxic than predicted or that it really doesn't work as anticipated.

Phase III clinical trials are designed to determine conclusively whether the drug being studied is effective when compared to the most effective drug already on the market. These studies are very large and sometimes include thousands of test subjects. The test sponsors might also use this phase to attempt to show that the drug may also be used for additional conditions beyond what the original application included. FDA guidelines actually allow a drug manufacturer to market the drug at this stage of testing if it meets the FDA requirements. However, if any new adverse effects or other problems arise once the drug is available to the public, the manufacturer is required to withdraw it from the market.

The next phase is known as the post-marketing surveillance trial or phase IV clinical trial. In this phase, the drug sponsor is responsible for ongoing technical support and safety surveillance of the drug after it has been marketed. In addition, the sponsor may be looking to show that a group not previously tested would benefit by using the drug for the condition for which it was originally intended. Since the drug is already on the market, there will be a very large patient study base and unusual long-term or rare adverse effects will be detected. If this occurs, the drug may be removed from the market or limited in its use.

NEW DRUGS BEING RESEARCHED TO TREAT CANCER

Much research is being performed in an effort to develop new anticancer medications. In some cases, the drugs are completely new classes that have not been used before. In other cases, the medications, or a form of them, are already on the market but used for a different condition. Testing merely finds that these drugs actually reduce tumor size or inhibit tumor growth. One such drug is a member of the bisphosphonate family. These drugs are generally used to treat osteoporosis and similar diseases because they help to prevent loss of bone mass.

Researchers in the University of Illinois chemistry department have had success with a new bisphosphonate called BPH-715.[2] A clinical trial using the bisphosphonate zoledronate in combination with hormone therapy significantly reduced the recurrence of breast cancer in premenopausal women with estrogen-receptor-positive breast cancer. Because this class of drugs is designed to bind to bone, however, its efficacy in other tissues was limited. This is where BPH-715 became useful.

University of Illinois chemist Rong Cao and Andrew Wang of Academia Sinica in Taipei, Taiwan, produced crystallographic structures of target enzymes in a tumor cell pathway. This allowed researchers to determine how to enhance a drug's ability to bind to these proteins rather than to bone. Using this information, University of Illinois chemist Yonghui Zhang created a bisphosphonate that bound to enzyme targets rather than bone. This made BPH-715 approximately 200 times more effective than zolendronate in killing cancer cells.

In a clinical trial designed to test an anticancer drug to be used in patients with a genetic predisposition, Dr. Johann de Bono used olaparib to treat breast, ovarian, and prostate cancers.[3] Women with gene mutations in the BRCA1 and BRCA2 genes have a higher incidence of breast and ovarian cancers than women without these gene mutations. Men with mutations in these genes have an increased risk of developing prostate cancer. Olaparib blocks poly(ADP-ribose) polymerase (PARP), a protein involved in DNA repair. Both healthy and cancer cells use PARP to repair themselves. Olaparib inhibits PARP, and cancer cells with the mutation in the BRCA gene are more sensitive to its actions.

In all the studies that de Bono conducted, side effects were minimal and the drug demonstrated strong anti-tumor activity. It was absorbed quickly and eliminated from the body in a short period of time. This aided in reducing side effects.

One of the most serious, painful, and extremely difficult to treat forms of cancer is pancreatic cancer. Another drug being tested is known as a TAK-1 inhibitor.[4] TAK-1 is a protein that helps cancer cells resist chemotherapy. By inhibiting this protein, cancer cells become more sensitive to standard forms of chemotherapy. Dr. Davide Melisi of the National Cancer Institute in Naples, Italy, was a researcher in a study on TAK-1. He explained that pancreatic cancer is incurable and resistant to every form of anticancer treatment. In this study, patients were given the TAK-1 inhibitor and then treated with the standard anticancer drugs Gemzar, Eloxatin, and Camptosar. The inhibitor increased the effectiveness of the chemotherapy drugs 70-fold.

Advanced metastatic castration-resistant, or hormone-refractory, prostate cancer is often a fatal condition. Although early stages of this cancer may be treated in a number of ways and cured, if left undetected they will become advanced. A phase III clinical trial was conducted to test the new experimental drug cabazitaxel.[5] The benefits were only moderate (prolonging life by several months), so at present, there are no treatments for this type of prostate cancer.

Cabazitaxel is a member of the drug class known as taxanes. It acts by inhibiting cell division in cancer cells. This drug was developed because docetaxel, another member of the taxane family that is the usual drug of choice for this type of cancer, eventually becomes ineffective as the prostate cancer cells develop a resistance to it. Cabazitaxel has the ability to elude the mechanism within prostate cancer cells that pumps out anticancer medications before they have the chance to do any damage to the cells.

On the positive side, men treated with cabazitaxel demonstrated an increased survival time without tumor growth and with significant shrinkage of the size of the tumors. Unfortunately, those treated with it experienced febrile neutropenia, which is a high fever associated with a significant decrease in white blood cells known as neutrophils. This could lead to a serious susceptibility to infections.

Cabazitaxel is not considered a first-choice treatment, but rather a second line of defense after treatment with drugs like docetaxel. The manufacturer, Sanofi-Aventis, will be seeking FDA approval as a second-line treatment. If granted, cabazitaxel would be the first drug to be classified in this manner.

The drugs just discussed are already in clinical trials and, if proven successful and reasonably safe, should be approved by the FDA in a reasonably short period of time. Other drugs whose development has only recently been completed will be ready to enter into clinical trials. There are literally thousands of clinical trials being conducted to determine whether or not proposed drugs for hundreds of conditions will meet the rigorous standards established by the FDA for approval.

Synta Pharmaceuticals Corporation is running a phase 1/2 (both phases at the same time) clinical trial of an experimental drug called STA-9090 that inhibits the heat shock protein HSP-90.[6] This is one of the most common heat shock proteins and is found in animals and bacteria. Its function in normal cells is to fold proteins and assist in intracellular transport, maintenance, and degradation of damaged or misfolded proteins. In cancer cells, HSP-90 stabilizes growth factor receptors and some signaling molecules. Its inhibition could lead to apoptosis (programmed cell death), thus killing cancer cells. It is also required for induction of vascular endothelial growth factor (VEGF) (see Chapter 5), so its inhibition would reduce the amount of blood vessels needed to sustain a tumor.

This clinical trial is designed to determine whether or not STA-9090 will be useful in treating three different types of leukemia; acute myeloid leukemia (AML), acute lymphoblastic leukemia (ALL), and chronic myelogenous leukemia (CML). The drug would be given once per week, so one of the factors being tested in this trial is the drug's safety with such frequent doses. Healthy individuals are not part of this study.

Another drug company, Onconova Therapeutics, is conducting a phase I clinical trial on a drug called ON 01910.Na, a Polo-like kinase 1 (Plk1) inhibitor. Plk1 is a **proto-oncogene** that is found in excessive amounts in tumor cells. In normal cells it aids in the mitotic process. Therefore, its inhibition could interfere with tumor cell mitosis, thus reducing tumor size. It is also found in excessively high quantities in refractory leukemia and myelodysplastic syndrome (MDS).[7]

Another clinical trial is being conducted with leukemia patients by Schering-Plough Corporation. In this study, participants with acute myelogenous leukemia (AML) will be randomized to receive SCH 727965 or gemtuzumab ozogamicin. All participants with acute lymphoblastic leukemia (ALL) will receive SCH 727965. Part 1 of the study will determine the activity of SCH 727965 treatment in participants with AML and participants with ALL. Part 2 of the study will determine the activity of SCH 727965 treatment in participants with AML who experienced disease progression after standard treatment with gemtuzumab ozogamicin during Part 1.[8]

SCH 727965 is an inhibitor of CDK1,2,5, and 9 proteins that are involved in cell division. Inhibiting these proteins will interfere with the normal division of leukemia cells as well as enhancing apoptosis.

The same manufacturer is also running a clinical trial using SCH 717454, an antibody that is directed against the insulin-like growth factor 1 receptor (IGF-1R). This receptor has been implicated in the growth and metastasis of several malignancies. This study is designed to determine whether SCH 717454 will improve the results obtained with the standard chemotherapy drugs temozolomide and irinotecan, or cyclophosphamide, doxorubicin, and vincristine, or ifosfamide and etoposide. The test subjects here will be children (21 years of age or younger) with advanced solid tumors.[9]

Combining experimental drugs with standard anticancer drugs is not a novel approach to treating cancers. It is hoped that the experimental drugs will enhance the cancer-fighting power of the traditional medicines. A clinical trial that involves CS 1008, a monoclonal antibody that appears to induce tumor cell apoptosis and a reduction in tumor growth, is being conducted. The drug will be used in combination with Sorafenib or the Sorafenib will be used alone to treat liver cancer. Once again, the trial participants must have the cancer and healthy individuals will not be part of the group.[10]

Stopping the growth of tumor cells by blocking blood flow to a tumor is crucial in reducing or eliminating the tumor. In a clinical study using AZD2171, a VEGF inhibitor, patients with locally advanced or metastatic liver cancer will be treated to determine the effectiveness of this drug. In addition to determining the efficacy of the drug, its safety is also being tested.

The test subjects will receive two regimens of the drug if, after the first, they are not exhibiting excessive toxicity and if the first regimen brought about improvement in their condition.[11]

The list of clinical trials is extensive, covering virtually every form of cancer in every age group. This is an indication of how important it is to health care practitioners and pharmaceutical companies alike to find safer, more effective treatments for a disease that ravages millions of people worldwide every year and has killed billions since humans first appeared on Earth. Studies are being carried out in almost every country throughout the world. Many are enjoying varying degrees of success and, with proper proof that the drugs being tested are reasonably safe and effective, the drug approval agencies of each country's government will be allowing the marketing of many new drugs in the future.

The sheer magnitude of the number of clinical trials, laboratories working day and night to find new, safer, more effective anticancer drugs, and the increase in awareness of what causes many forms of cancer, will surely bring hope to humanity that one day, this scourge may be eliminated.

Notes

Chapter 1

1. Will Dunham, "Cancer Death Rate Down, but 565,650 Seen in 2008," Reuters, February 20, 2008, http://www.reuters.com/article/newsOne/idUSN1926392720080220 (accessed September 22, 2009); Cancer Research UK, "Cancer Worldwide: The Global Picture," http://info.cancerresearchuk.org/cancerstats/geographic/world (accessed September 22, 2009).

2. Jules Hirsch, "An Anniversary for Cancer Chemotherapy," *Journal of the American Medical Association* 296, 12 (September 27, 2006): pp. 1518–1520, http://jama.ama-assn.org/cgi/content/full/296/12/1518 (accessed on September 22, 2009).

3. L.S. Goodman, M.M. Wintrobe, W. Dameshek, et al., (1984). "Landmark Article Sept. 21, 1946: Nitrogen Mustard Therapy. Use of Methyl-Bis (Beta-Chloroethyl) Amine Hydrochloride and Tris(Beta-Chloroethyl) Amine Hydrochloride for Hodgkin's Disease, Lymphosarcoma, Leukemia and Certain Allied and Miscellaneous Disorders," *Journal of the American Medical Association* 251 (17): 2255–2261.

4. Bert Vogelstein and Kenneth W. Kinzler, *The Genetic Basis of Human Cancer* (New York: McGraw-Hill, 2002).

5. National Cancer Institute, "What You Need to Know About Cancer—An Overview: Risk Factors," http://www.cancer.gov/cancertopics/wyntk/overview/page4 (accessed on September 24, 2009).

6. Toren Finkel, Manuel Serrano, and Maria A. Blasco, "The Common Biology of Cancer and Ageing," *Nature* 448 (August 16, 2007), http://www.nature.com/nature/journal/v448/n7155/full/nature05985.html (accessed September 24, 2009); America's Seniors, "Cancer and Aging: New findings in Yeast May Help Reveal Why Growing Older

Is the Greatest Carcinogen in Humans," Today's Seniors Network, September 25, 2003, http://www.todaysseniors network.com/Aging%20 and%20Cancer.htm (accessed September 25, 2009).

7. American Cancer Society, "Tobacco and Cancer," http://www.cancer.org/docroot/PED/ped_10.asp. (accessed September 25, 2009).

8. National Cancer Institute, "Smoking," http://www.cancer.gov/cancertopics/smoking (accessed September 25, 2009).

9. Canadian Centre for Occupational Health and Safety, "Skin Cancer and Sunlight," http://www.ccohs.ca/oshanswers/diseases/skin_cancer.html (accessed September September 25, 2009).

10. National Cancer Institute, "BRCA1 and BRCA2: Cancer Risk and Genetic Testing," http://www.cancer.gov/cancer topics/factsheet/Risk/BRCA#2 (accessed September 29, 2009).

11. National Cancer Institute, "Obesity and Cancer: Questions and Answers," http://www.cancer.gov/cancertopics/factsheet/Risk/obesity (accessed September 29, 2009).

12. Ibid.

13. Cancer Research UK, "Diet Causing Cancer," March 4, 2009, http://www.cancer help.org.uk/help/default.asp?page=120#foodadd (accessed September 29, 2009).

14. See note 11 above.

15. National Cancer Institute, "Cancer Causes and Risk Factors," http://www.cancer.gov/cancertopics/prevention-genetics-causes/causes (accessed September 30, 2009; Sid Kirchheimer, "Herpes Virus Linked to Cervical Cancer: Appears to be 'Accomplice' with Other Virus," WebMD, November 5, 2002, http://www.webmd.com/genital-herpes/guide/20061101/herpes-virus-linked-to-cervical-cancer (accessed September 30, 2009).

16. University of Iowa Hospitals and Clinics, "Health Topics: Viruses and Cancer," May 2003, http://www.uihealthcare.com/topics/medicaldepartments/cancercenter/cancer tips/viruses.html (accessed September 30, 2009); Cancer Research UK, "What Causes Cancer?" March 9, 2009, http://www.cancerhelp.org.uk/help/default.asp?page=119#viruses (accessed September 30, 2009).

Chapter 2

1. Chemical Heritage Foundation, "Cancer Chemotherapy: A Timeline. Magic Bullets:

Chemistry vs. Cancer," http://www.chemheritage.org/educationalservices/pharm/chemo/readings/timeline.htm (accessed October 6, 2009).

2. Diane M. Murphy, "Cancer Chemotherapy History," eHow, http://www.ehow.com/about_5078583_cancer-chemotherapy-history.html (accessed October 6, 2009); John M. Riddle, "Ancient and Medieval Chemotherapy for Cancer," *Isis* 76, 3 (September 1985): 319–330, http://www.jstor.org/stable/232855 (accessed October 7, 2009); Chemical Heritage Foundation, "Cancer Chemotherapy: A Chemical Needle in a Haystack," http://www.chemheritage.org/educationalservices/pharm/chemo/readings/ages.htm (accessed October 7, 2009).

3. William B. Coley, "The Treatment of Malignant Tumors by Repeated Inoculations of Erysipelas: With a Report of Ten Original Cases," *American Journal of the Medical Sciences* 10 (1893): 487–511.

4. Cancer Decisions, "Announcing New Report on Coley's Toxins," April 19, 2009, http://www.cancerdecisions.com/content/view/184/2/lang,english/ (accessed August 8, 2010).

5. Sidney Farber, et al., "Temporary Remissions in Acute Leukemia in Children Produced by Folic Antagonist 4-Aminopteroylglutamic Acid," *New England Journal of Medicine* 238 (1948): 787–793.

6. Min Chiu Li, Roy Hertz, and Delbert M. Bergenstal, "Therapy of Choriocarcinoma and Related Trophoblastic Tumors with Folic Acid and Purine Antagonists," *New England Journal of Medicine* 259 (1958): 66–74.

7. Marshall A. Lichtman, et al. (eds), *Hematology: Landmark Papers of the Twentieth Century* (San Diego, Calif.: Academic Press, 2000).

8. Gianni Bonadonnna, et al., "Combination Chemotherapy as an Adjuvant Treatment in Operable Breast Cancer," *New England Journal of Medicine* 294 (1976): 405–410.

9. Barnett Rosenberg, Loretta Van Camp, and Thomas Krigas, "Inhibition of Cell Division in *Escherichia coli* by Electrolysis Products from a Platinum Electrode," *Nature* 205 (1965): 698–699.

10. Thomas P. Johnston, George S. McCaleb, and John A. Montgomery. "The Synthesis of Antineoplastic Agents. XXXII. N-Nitrosoureas." *Journal*

of Medicinal Chemistry 6, 6 (November 1963): 669–681.

11. Drugs.com, "Fludarabine Phosphate," http://www.drugs.com/ppa/fludarabine-phosphate.html (accessed October 16, 2009).

12. Rachel Ann Clark, Suzanne Snedeker, and Carol Devine, "Estrogen and Breast Cancer Risk: The Relationship," *Program on Breast Cancer and Environmental Risk Factors,* Cornell University, March 1998, http://envirocancer.cornell.edu/FactSheet/General/fs9.estrogen.cfm (accessed October 19, 2009).

13. National Cancer Institute, "Tamoxifen: Questions and Answers," http://www.cancer.gov/cancertopics/factsheet/Therapy/tamoxifen (accessed October 19, 2009).

14. Genentech/Biogen Idec, "Rituxan: Proposed Mechanism of Action," http://www.rituxan.com/lymphoma/hcp/MOA/index.m (accessed October 19, 2009).

Chapter 3

1. National Cancer Institute, "A to Z List of Cancers," http://www.cancer.gov/cancertopics/alphalist (accessed October 26, 2009.

2. Non-Hodgkin's Lymphoma Centers, "Glossary of Terms," http://www.patientcenters.com/lymphoma/news/nhl7.html (accessed October 29, 2009.

3. The Children's Hospital of Philadelphia, "Health Information: Skin Cancer," 2007, http://www.chop.edu/healthinfo/skin-cancer.html (accessed November 3, 2009; C.S.M. Wong, R.C. Strange, and T. Lear, "Basal Cell Carcinoma," *British Medical Journal* 327 (October 2003): 794–798, http://www.bmj.com/cgi/content/extract/327/7418/794 (accessed November 3, 2009).

4. American Cancer Society, "Treating Basal Cell Carcinoma," June 10, 2008. http://www.cancer.org/docroot/CRI/content/CRI_2_4_4X_Treatment_of_Basal_Cell_Carcinoma_51.asp?rnav=cri (accessed November 3, 2009).

5. National Cancer Institute, "Bladder Cancer Treatment," http://www.cancer.gov/cancertopics/pdq/treatment/bladder/HealthProfessional/page2 (accessed November 3, 2009).

6. National Cancer Institute, "Bone Cancer: Questions and Answers," http://www.cancer.gov/cancertopics/factsheet/Sites-Types/bone (accessed November 5, 2009).

7. Marilena Cesari, et al., "Mesenchymal Chondrosarcoma:

An Analysis of Patients Treated at a Single Institution," *Tumori* 93 (2007): 423–427, http://www.tumorionline.it/allegati/00304_2007_05/fulltext/03%20Cesari%20%28423-427%29.pdf (accessed November 6, 2009).

8. St. Jude's Children's Research Hospital, "Solid Tumor: Ewing Sarcoma Family Tumors," http://www.stjude.org/stjude/v/index.jsp?vgnextoid=174c061585f70110VgnVCM1000001e0215acRCRD&vgnextchannel=bc4fbfe82e118010VgnVCM1000000e2015acRCRD (accessed November 9, 2009).

9. National Cancer Institute, "Brain Tumor," http://www.cancer.gov/cancertopics/types/brain (accessed on November 10, 2009).

10. National Cancer Institute, "Post-Surgical Treatment for Childhood Low-Grade Astrocytomas," http://www.cancer.gov/cancertopics/pdq/treatment/child-astrocytomas/HealthProfessional/page9 (accessed November 10, 2009); Massachusetts General Hospital Brain Tumor Center, "A Guide to Chemotherapy for Brain Tumor Patients," http://brain.mgh.harvard.edu/ChemoGuide.htm (accessed November 10, 2009).

11. National Cancer Institute, "Breast Cancer," http://www.cancer.gov/cancertopics/types/breast (accessed November 10, 2009).

12. National Cancer Institute, "Cervical Cancer," http://www.cancer.gov/cancertopics/types/cervical (accessed November 12, 2009).

13. American Cancer Society, "Detailed Guide: Cervical Cancer Chemotherapy." http://www.cancer.org/docroot/CRI/content/CRI_2_4_4X_Chemotherapy_8.asp (accessed November 12, 2009).

14. National Cancer Institute, "Colon and Rectal Cancer," http://www.cancer.gov/cancertopics/types/colon-and-rectal (accessed November 12, 2009).

15. Jose Iscovich, et al., "Classic Kaposi's Sarcoma in Jews Living in Israel, 1961–1989: A Population-Based Incidence Study." *AIDS* 12, 15 (1998): 2067–2072, http://journals.lww.com/aidsonline/pages/articleviewer.aspx?year=1998&issue=15000&article=00019&type=abstract (accessed November 14, 2009); Eyal Fenig, et al., "Classic Kaposi Sarcoma: Experience at Rabin Medical Center in Israel," *American Journal of Clinical Oncology* 21, 5 (1998): 498–

500, http://journals.lww.com/
amjclinicaloncology/pages/
articleviewer.aspx?year=1998
&issue=10000&article=00016
&type=abstract (accessed
November 14, 2009); P. Cook-
Mozaffari, "The Geographi-
cal Distribution of Kaposi's
Sarcoma and of Lymphomas
in Africa Before the AIDS
Epidemic," *British Journal
of Cancer* 78, 11 (Decem-
ber 1998): 1521–1528; S.J.
Olsen, "Increasing Kaposi's
Sarcoma-Associated Herpesvirus Seroprevalence with Age
in a Highly Kaposi's Sarcoma
Endemic Region, Zambia in
1985," *AIDS* 12, 14 (October
1998): 1921–1925.

16. Robert A. Schwartz and
W. Clark Lambert, "Kaposi
Sarcoma," emedicine,
June 18, 2010, http://
emedicine.medscape.com/
article/1083998-overview
(accessed August 10, 2010).

17. Lymphoma Research Foundation, "Understanding CLL/
SLL," http://www.lymphoma.
org/atf/cf/%7B0363cdd6-51b5-
427b-be48-e6af871acec9%7D/
CLL_SLL10.PDF#page=46
(accessed August 24, 2010).

18. Flavio Guzman, "Imatinib
(Gleevec) pharmacology:
mechanism of action and
therapeutic considerations,"

Pharmacology Corner,
November 20, 2008, http://
pharmacologycorner.com/
imatinib-mechanism-of-actio/
(accessed August 24, 2010).

19. CancerHelp UK, "Chemotherapy Drugs for Hodgkin's lymphoma and Their Side Effects,"
http://www.cancerhelp.org.
uk/type/hodgkins-lymphoma/
treatment/chemotherapy/
chemotherapy-drugs-for-
hodgkins-lymphoma-and-
their-side-effects (accessed
November 18, 2009).

20. LymphomaInfo.net, "Non-
Hodgkin's Lymphoma:
Chemotherapy," http://www.
lymphomainfo.net/nhl/chemo.
html (accessed November 18,
2009).

21. National Cancer Institute,
"Melanoma," http://www.
cancer.gov/cancertopics/types/
melanoma (accessed November
18, 2009.

22. Google Health, "Multiple
Myeloma," https://health.
google.com/health/ref/
Multiple+myeloma#Treatment
(accessed November 19, 2009).

23. National Cancer Institute,
"Ovarian Cancer," http://www.
cancer.gov/cancertopics/types/
ovarian (accessed November
19, 2009).

24. American Cancer Society,
"Detailed Guide: Ovarian

Cancer Chemotherapy," http://
www.cancer.org/docroot/
CRI/content/CRI_2_4_4X_
Chemotherapy_33.asp
(accessed November 19, 2009).

25. National Cancer Institute,
"Pancreatic Cancer." http://
www.cancer.gov/cancertopics/
types/pancreatic (accessed
November 19, 2009).

26. American Cancer Society,
"Detailed Guide: Pancreatic
Cancer Chemotherapy," http://
www.cancer.org/docroot/
CRI/content/CRI_2_4_4X_
Chemotherapy_34.asp
(accessed November 19, 2009).

27. National Cancer Institute,
"Prostate Cancer," http://www.
cancer.gov/cancertopics/pdq/
treatment/prostate/Health
Professional/page2 (accessed
November 19, 2009).

Chapter 4

1. Charles E. Ophardt, "Anti-
Cancer Drugs I and II,"
Virtual Chembook. Elmhurst
College, 2003, http://
www.elmhurst.edu/~chm/
vchembook/655cancer.html
(accessed December 8, 2009).

2. Non-Hodgkin's Lymphoma
Cyberfamily, "Chemotherapy,"
http://www.nhlcyberfamily.
org/treatments/chemotherapy.
htm (accessed December 8,
2009).

3. University of California, San
Francisco Medical Center,
"Immunosuppression and Cancer," http://www.dermatology.
ucsf.edu/skincancer/transplant/
Immunosuppression.aspx
(accessed December 8, 2009).

4. Non-Hodgkin's Lymphoma
Cyberfamily, "Side Effects
From Treatment," http://www.
nhlcyberfamily.org/treatments/
effects.htm (accessed December 9, 2009).

5. American Cancer Society,
"What Causes Side Effects?"
http://www.cancer.org/
docroot/MBC/content/
MBC_2_2X_What_Causes_
Side_Effects.asp?sitearea=MBC
(accessed December 9, 2009).

Chapter 5

1. National Cancer Institute,
"Bevacizumab (Avastin) for
Treatment of Solid Tumors,"
http://www.cancer.gov/cancer
topics/factsheet/therapy/avastin
(accessed January 14, 2010).

2. American Cancer Society, "How
Anti-angiogenesis Drugs
Work," http://www.cancer.
org/docroot/ETO/content/
ETO_1_4X_The_Details_
How_Antiangiogenesis_
Drugs_Work.asp?sitearea=ETO
(accessed January 14, 2010).

3. National Cancer Institute,
"Biological Therapies for

Cancer: Questions and Answers," http://www.cancer. gov/cancertopics/factsheet/ Therapy/biological (accessed January 27, 2010).

4. National Cancer Institute. "COX-2 Inhibitors and Cancer." Available online. URL: http://www.cancer.gov/cancer topics/factsheet/prevention/ cox-2-inhibitors (accessed January 27, 2010).

5. Irving J. Lerner, "Laetrile: A Lesson in Cancer Quackery," *CA: A Cancer Journal for Clinicians* 31 (1981): 91–95.

6. Nicholas Wade, "Laetrile at Sloan-Kettering: A Question of Ambiguity," *Science* 198, 4323 (December 23, 1977): 1231–1234.

7. Ibid.

8. CERBE Distribution, Inc., "714-X: Technical Data," http:// www.cerbe.com/en/techdata. pdf (accessed January 31, 2010).

9. Stanislaw R. Burzynski, "Antineoplastons: History of the Research," *Drugs Under Experimental and Clinical Research* 12, suppl. 1 (1986): 1–9.

10. Stanislaw R. Burzynski, "Purified Antineoplaston Fractions and Methods of Treating Neoplastic Disease," U.S. Patent 4558057, December 10, 1985, Washington, D.C.: US. Patent and Trademark Office, http://

patft.uspto.gov/netacgi/nphPa rser?Sect1=PTO1&Sect2=HIT OFF&d=PALL&p=1&u=%2Fn etahtml%2FPTO%2Fsrchnum. htm&r=1&f=G&l=50&s1= 4558057.PN.&OS=PN/ 4558057&RS=PN/4558057 (accessed January 31, 2010).

11. S. Green, "Antineoplastons: An Unproved Cancer Therapy," *Journal of the American Medical Association* 267, 1 (June 3, 1992), http://caonline.amcancer soc.org/cgi/reprint/31/2/91 (accessed January 31, 2010).

12. National Cancer Institute, "Cartilage (Bovine and Shark)," http://www.cancer. gov/cancertopics/pdq/cam/ cartilage/HealthProfessional/ page2 (accessed January 31, 2010); C.L. Loprinzi, et al., "Evaluation of Shark Cartilage in Patients with Advanced Cancer: A North Central Cancer Treatment Group Trial," *Cancer* 104, 1 (2005): 176–182.

13. D. Iarussi, et al., "Protective Effect of Coenzyme Q10 on Anthracyclines Cardiotoxicity: Control Study in Children with Acute Lymphoblastic Leukemia and Non-Hodgkin Lymphoma," *Molecular Aspects of Medicine* 15 (1994): S207; K. Folkers, et al., "Increase in Levels of IgG in Serum of Patients Treated with

Coenzyme Q10," *Research Communications in Chemical Pathology and Pharmacology* 38, 2 (1982): 335–338; K. Lockwood, S. Moesgaard, and K. Folkers, "Partial and Complete Regression of Breast Cancer in Patients in Relation to Dosage of Coenzyme Q10," *Biochemical and Biophysical Research Communications* 199, 3 (1994): 1504–1508.

14. K. Folkers, et al., "Inhibition of Two Human Tumor Cell Lines by Antimetabolites of Coenzyme Q10," *Research Communications in Chemical Pathology and Pharmacology* 19, 3 (1978): 485–490.

15. G. Buchbauer, et al., "Fragrance Compounds and Essential Oils with Sedative Effects upon Inhalation," *Journal of Pharmaceutical Sciences* 82, 6 (1993): 660–664.

16. S.M. Wilkinson, et al., "Effectiveness of Aromatherapy Massage in the Management of Anxiety and Depression in Patients with Cancer: A Multicenter Randomized Controlled Trial," *Journal of Clinical Oncology* 25, 5 (2007): 532–539; J. Stringer, "Massage and Aromatherapy on a Leukaemia Unit," *Complementary Therapies in Nursing and Midwifery* 6, 2 (2000): 72–76.

17. National Cancer Institute, "Essiac/Flor·Essence," http://www.cancer.gov/cancertopics/pdq/cam/essiac/HealthProfessional/page3#Reference3.1 (accessed February 2, 2010).

18. C. Tamayo, et al. "The Chemistry and Biological Activity of Herbs Used in Flor-Essence Herbal Tonic and Essiac." *Phytotherapy Research* 14 (1), pp. 1–14, 2000; E. Kaegi, "Unconventional Therapies for Cancer: 1. Essiac. The Task Force on Alternative Therapies of the Canadian Breast Cancer Research Initiative." *Canadian Medical Association Journal* 158, 7 (1998): 897–902.

19. J. Ottenweller, et al. "Inhibition of Prostate Cancer-Cell Proliferation by Essiac." *Journal of Alternative and Complimentary Medicine* 10, 4 (2004): 687–691.

20. L.M. Bennett, et al. "Flor-Essence Herbal Tonic Does Not Inhibit Mammary Tumor Development in Sprague Dawley Rats." *Breast Cancer Research and Treatment* 88, 1 (2004), pp. 87–93.

21. K.S. Kulp, et al. "Essiac and Flor-Essence Herbal Tonics Stimulate the In Vitro Growth of Human Breast Cancer Cells." *Breast Cancer Research and Treatment* 98, 3 (2006): 249–259.

22. J. Tai, et al., "In Vitro Comparison of Essiac and Flor·Essence on human tumor cell lines." *Oncology Reports* 11, 2 (2004): 471–476.

23. National Cancer Institute, "Essiac/Flor·Essence," http://www.cancer.gov/cancertopics/pdq/cam/essiac/HealthProfessional/page3#Reference3.1 (accessed February 2, 2010).

Chapter 6

1. Gloria S. Ross, "Melanie Shouse: Activist for Health Care," *St. Louis Beacon,* February 6, 2010, http://www.stlbeacon.org/content/view/100109/483 (accessed February 17, 2010).

2. Anna Werner, "Insurance Won't Pay NorCal Mom's Cancer Treatment," Local News, CBS 5 San Francisco, May 12, 2009, http://cbs5.com/local/cancer.treatment.denied.2.1007394.html (accessed February 9, 2010.

3. Andrew Pollack, "Questioning a $30,000-a-Month Cancer Drug," *The New York Times,* December 4, 2009, http://www.nytimes.com/2009/12/05/health/05drug.html (accessed February 17, 2010); Eric Jacobson and Arnold S. Friedman, "Treatment of Relapsed or Refractory Peripheral T-cell Lymphoma," UpToDate for Patients, http://www.uptodateonline.com/patients/content/topic.do?topicKey=~oClyo2F8GXs8AzC (accessed February 17, 2010).

4. Neal Masia, "The Cost of Developing a New Drug," U.S. Department of State, April 23, 2008, http://www.america.gov/st/econ-english/2008/April/20080429230904myleen0.5233981.html (accessed February 19, 2010).

5. David W. Tschanz, "Arab Roots of European Medicine," *Heart Views,* 4, 2 (August 2003); D. Craig Brater and Walter J. Daly, "Clinical Pharmacology in the Middle Ages: Principles That Presage the 21st Century," *Clinical Pharmacology and Therapeutics* 67, 5 (2000): 447–450.

6. Tito Fojo and Christine Grady, "How Much Is Life Worth? Cetuximab, Non-Small-Cell Lung Cancer, and the $440 Billion Question," *Journal of the National Cancer Institute* 101 (June 30, 2009): 1–5.

7. Nick Mulcahy, "Time to Consider Cost in Evaluating Cancer Drugs in the United States?" Medscape Infectious Diseases, July 14, 2009, http://www.medscape.com/viewarticle/705689 (accessed February 20, 2010).

8. Fox Chase Cancer Center, "Can We Afford the Cancer Care of the Future?" *ScienceDaily*, May 27, 2009, http://www.sciencedaily.com/releases/2009/05/090526140751.htm (accessed February 20, 2010).

9. Jeffrey Norris, "Cancer Drug Costs May Be Unbearable, Even for Insured," *Science Café*, University of California, San Francisco, February 10, 2009, http://www.ucsf.edu/science-cafe/conversations/cancer-drug-cost-may-be-unbearable-even-for-insured/ (accessed February 23, 2010).

10. Victoria Colliver, "Study Points to Cancer's Financial Malignancy," *The San Francisco Chronicle*, February 6, 2009, http://www.sfgate.com/cgi-bin/article.cgi?f=/c/a/2009/02/06/MN9T15LLN4.DTL (accessed February 23, 2010).

11. New York Presbyterian Hospital, "State Legislation," *Cancer Prevention*, 2010, http://www.nypcancerprevention.com/issue/14/cancer_prevention/leg/state-legislation-2.shtml (accessed February 23, 2010).

12. California HealthCare Foundation, "Panel Approves Bill to Equalize Coverage for zChemotherapy Drugs," *California Healthline*, July 8, 2009, http://www.californiahealthline.org/articles/2009/7/8/panel-approves-bill-to-equalize-coverage-for-chemotherapy-drugs.aspx (accessed February 23, 2010).

13. *USA Today*/Kaiser Family Foundation/Harvard School of Public Health, *National Survey of Households Affected by Cancer*, November 2006, http://kff.org/kaiserpolls/upload/7590.pdf (accessed February 23, 2010).

14. Neal J. Meropol, et al., "American Society of Clinical Oncology Guidance Statement: The Cost of Cancer Care," *Journal of Clinical Oncology* 27, July 6, 2009, http://jco.ascopubs.org/cgi/reprint/JCO.2009.23.1183v1 (accessed on February 23, 2010); J.M. Hoffman, et al., "Projecting Future Drug Expenditures—2009," *American Journal of Health-System Pharmacy* 66, 3 (2009): 237–257.

15. See note 13 above.

16. S. Keehan, et al., "Health Spending Projections Through 2017: The Baby-Boom Generation Is Coming to Medicare," *Health Affairs* 27, 2 (February 26, 2008): w145–w155.

Chapter 7

1. U.S. Food and Drug Administration, "How Drugs are

Developed and Approved,"
http://www.fda.gov/Drugs/
DevelopmentApprovalProcess/
HowDrugsareDeveloped
andApproved/default.htm
(accessed March 14, 2010).

2. University of Illinois at
Urbana-Champaign, "New
Anti-Cancer Drug: 200 Times
More Active in Killing Tumor
Cells," *ScienceDaily,* March 26,
2009, http://www.sciencedaily.
com /releases/2009/03/
090325132458.htm (accessed
March 14, 2010).

3. HealthDay News, "New
Cancer Drug Fights Tumors
in Those with BRCA Muta-
tions," June 24, 2009, http://
news.health.com/2009/06/25/
new-cancer-drug-fights-
tumors-those-brca-mutations/
(accessed August 24, 2010).

4. Charlene Laino, "New Drug
May Treat Pancreatic Can-
cer: Experimental Treatment
Improves the Effective-
ness of Chemotherapy,"
WebMD, September 24, 2009,
http://www.webmd.com/
cancer/pancreatic-cancer/
news/20090924/new-drug-
may-treat-pancreatic-cancer
(accessed March 14, 20100.

5. Edward R. Winstead and Carmen Phillips, "Experimental
Drug Benefits Patients with
Advanced Prostate Cancer,"
NCI Cancer Bulletin, March 9,
2010, http://www.cancer.gov/
ncicancerbulletin/030910/
page2 (accessed March 15,
2010).

6. National Institutes of Health,
"A Phase 1/2 Study of the
HSP90 Inhibitor, STA-9090,
Administered Once Weekly
in Subjects with Acute
Myeloid Leukemia, Acute
Lymphoblastic Leukemia
and Blast-phase Chronic
Myelogenous Leukemia,"
ClinicalTrialsFeeds.org,
December 10, 2009, http://
clinicaltrialsfeeds.org/clinical-
trials/show/NCT00964873
(accessed March 15, 2010).

7. National Institutes of Health,
"Phase I Dose Escalation
Study of ON 01910.Na with
Increasing Duration of an
Initial 3-Day Continuous
Infusion in Patients with
Refractory Leukemia or Myelo-
dysplastic Syndrome (MDS),"
ClinicalTrialsFeeds.org,
January 26, 2010, http://clinical
trialsfeeds.org/clinical-trials/
show/NCT00854646 (accessed
March 15, 2010); T. Ikezoe,
et al., "A Novel Treatment Strat-
egy Targeting Polo-like Kinase
1 in Hematological Malig-
nancies," *Cell Cycle Research*,
May 7, 2009, http://www.
cellcycles.org/showabstract.

php?pmid=19421227 (accessed March 15, 2010).

8. National Institutes of Health, "A Phase 2 Study of SCH 727965 in Subjects with Relapsed and Refractory Acute Myelogenous Leukemia and Acute Lymphoblastic Leukemia," ClinicalTrialsFeeds. org, February 9, 2010, http:// clinicaltrialsfeeds.org/clinical-trials/show/NCT00798213 (accessed March 15, 2010).

9. National Institutes of Health, "A Phase 1/1B Dose-Escalation Study to Determine the Safety and Tolerability of SCH 717454 Administered in Combination with Chemotherapy in Pediatric Subjects with Advanced Solid Tumors (Protocol No. 05883)," ClinicalTrialsFeeds. org, March 11, 2010, http:// clinicaltrialsfeeds.org/

clinical-trials/show/ NCT00960063 (accessed March 15, 2010).

10. National Institutes of Health, "Clinical Study Protocol Phase 2, Randomized Study of CS-1008 in Combination with Sorafenib Compared to Sorafenib Alone as First-Line Systemic Therapy in Subjects with Advanced Hepatocellular Carcinoma," ClinicalTrialsFeeds.org, March 10, 2010, http://clinicaltrialsfeeds. org/clinical-trials/show/ NCT01033240 (accessed March 15, 2010).

11. National Institutes of Health, "A Phase II Study of AZD2171 in Hepatocellular Carcinoma," ClinicalTrialsFeeds.org, June 16, 2009, http://clinicaltrials feeds.org/clinical-trials/show/ NCT00427973 (accessed March 15, 2010).

Glossary

adjuvant therapy   Treatment given after primary treatment for a cancer that is intended to increase long-term survival.

angiogenesis   The formation of new blood vessels.

antioxidant   A substance capable of counteracting the damage caused by oxidation in animal tissue.

apoptosis   Genetically programmed self-destruction of a cell characterized by fragmentation of nuclear DNA.

astrocyte   A star-shaped neuroglial cell that supports neurons in the central nervous system.

bisphosphonates   A group of carbon-substituted analogues of pyrophosphate that inhibits the activity of osteoclasts in reabsorbing bone.

camphor   A ketone derived from the camphor tree used to treat pain and itching and as a counterirritant for infections.

carcinogen   A chemical or other substance that causes cancer.

cathartic   A chemical that cleans out the bowels.

cryosurgery   A procedure that uses extreme cold to destroy tissue. Liquid nitrogen is often used as the extremely cold substance. Also known as cryotherapy.

electrodesiccation   The drying of tissue with a high-frequency electric current introduced via a needle-shaped electrode.

ependymal cells   Neuroglial cells in the brain that are responsible for the production of cerebrospinal fluid.

erysipelas   An acute infectious disease caused by *Streptococcus pyogenes* that is accompanied by a fever and associated with a spreading deep red inflammation of the mucous membranes or the skin.

formaldehyde   A potentially carcinogenic chemical used as a disinfectant and preservative and in the manufacture of resins and plastics.

heterocyclic amines Carcinogenic chemicals formed when amino acids and creatine (a muscle protein) react at high cooking temperatures, as in frying.

ionizing radiation High-energy radiation that produces ions in any substance through which it passes.

ions Electrically charged atoms or groups of atoms that have lost or gained electrons.

lymphoma A malignant tumor that arises in any of the lymph tissues.

malignant Growing uncontrollably and displaying invasive characteristics.

metastasis When cancer cells spread from their original site to a distant site or sites via the bloodstream, lymphatic system, or across membranous surfaces.

microglia Phagocytic neuroglial cells in the central nervous system that protect against invading microorganisms and remove dead tissue.

neo-adjuvant therapy Treatment given before primary therapy for treating a cancerous tumor. It is designed to shrink the tumor, thus making surgery easier.

nitrosamines Neutral compounds containing the group NNO (nitrogen, nitrogen, oxygen) that are known to cause cancer in many cases.

oligodendrocyte A neuroglial cell with few branches that wraps around neurons in the central nervous system and protects them with myelin.

oncogene A gene that causes the formation of a cancerous growth.

placebo A substance that has no pharmacological or therapeutic effect but is used as a control when testing another substance for efficacy in treating a specific condition.

proto-oncogene A normally present gene that regulates normal cell growth. Due to mutation, it may be transformed into an oncogene.

senescent Old; aged.

targeted therapy The use of a medication that is designed to block the growth of cancer cells by interfering with specific targeted molecules needed for carcinogenesis.

tumor suppressor genes Genes that protect cells from becoming cancerous. The are also called anti-oncogenes.

further Resources

Books and Articles

The American Cancer Society. *Breast Cancer Clear and Simple: All Your Questions Answered*. Atlanta: The American Cancer Society, 2007.

The American Cancer Society. *Cancer: What Causes It, What Doesn't*. Atlanta: The American Cancer Society, 2003.

The American Cancer Society. *Good for You! Reducing Your Risk of Developing Cancer*. Atlanta: The American Cancer Society, 2002.

The American Cancer Society. *Lung Cancer: What You Need to Know—NOW!* Atlanta: The American Cancer Society, 2007.

Anderson, Greg. *Cancer: 50 Essential Things to Do*. New York: Penguin, 1999.

Avendano, Carmen, and J. Carlos Menendez. *Medicinal Chemistry of Anticancer Drugs*. Amsterdam: Elsevier, 2008.

Buolamwini, John, and Alex Adjei (eds.). *Novel Anticancer Drug Protocols*. New York: Humana Press, 2007.

Cragg, Gordon M., et al. (eds.). *Anticancer Agents from Natural Products*. Boca Raton, Fla.: CRC Press, 2005.

Goodman, Jordan, and Vivien Walsh. *The Story of Taxol: Nature and Politics in the Pursuit of an Anticancer Drug*. Cambridge, U.K.: Cambridge University Press, 2006.

Henderson, Bill. *Cancer-Free: Your Guide to Gentle, Non-toxic Healing*. 3rd ed. N.P.: Booklocker.com, 2007.

Keane, Maureen, and Daniella Chace. *What to Eat If You Have Cancer: Healing Foods That Boost Your Immune System*. New York: McGraw-Hill, 2007.

Mackay, Judith, M.D., et al. *The Cancer Atlas*. Atlanta: The American Cancer Society, 2006.

Mehta, Kapil, and Zahid Siddik (eds.). *Drug Resistance in Cancer Cells*. New York: Springer, 2009.

Neidle, Stephen (ed.). *Cancer Drug Design and Discovery*. New York: Elsevier, 2007.

Ozols, Robert F. (ed.). *Molecular and Clinical Advances in Anticancer Drug Resistance*. Dordrecht, Netherlands: Kluwer Academic, 2009.

Servan-Schreiber, David. *Anticancer: A New Way of Life*. New York: Penguin, 2008.

Spencer, Peter, and Walter Holt (eds.). *Anticancer Drugs: Design, Delivery and Pharmacology*. Waltham, Mass.: Nova Biomedical, 2009.

Web Sites

BioInfoBank Library: Recent Patents on Anti-cancer Drug Discovery
http://lib.bioinfo.pl/pmid/journal/Recent%20Pat%20Anticancer%20
Drug%20Discov

BiotechDaily: Tumor-Homing Peptide Enhances Delivery of Anticancer Drugs
http://biotechdaily.com/?option=com_article&Itemid=294726984&
cat=Genomics/Protemics

Drugs.com: What is Cancer?
http://www.drugs.com/cancer.html

e! Science News: Fatty Acid to Enhance Anticancer Drug
http://esciencenews.com/articles/2010/05/07/fatty.acid.enhance.
anticancer.drug

Healthline: Anticancer Drugs
http://www.healthline.com/galecontent/anticancer-drugs

Highlights in Chemical Biology: Pairing Up Against Cancer
http://www.rsc.org/Publishing/Journals/cb/Volume/2010/05/novel_
approach.asp

Highlights in Chemical Science: Three Steps to Potential Anticancer Drugs
http://www.rsc.org/Publishing/ChemScience/Volume/2010/06/
three_step_synthesis.asp

Livestrong.com: Anti-Cancer Drugs to Treat Breast Cancer
http://www.livestrong.com/article/92370-anticancer-drugs-treat-
    breast-cancer/

medGadget: Nanosponges Carrying Anticancer Drugs Effectively Slow
    Tumor Growth
http://medgadget.com/archives/2010/06/nanosponges_carrying_
    anticancer_drugs_effectively_slow_tumor_growth.html

Reefkeeping: Anticancer Drugs from the Coral Reef: Prospects and
    Promise
http://reefkeeping.com/issues/2006-11/kf/index.phpCancer

ScienceDaily: New Anti-Cancer Drug: 200 Times More Active in Killing
    Tumor Cells
http://www.sciencedaily.com/releases/2009/03/090325132458.htm

Scientific American: Cancer Drugs May Also Treat Alcoholism
http://www.scientificamerican.com/podcast/episode.cfm?id=
    cancer-drugs-may-also-treat-alcholi-09-05-26

Index

About the Author

Dr. Alan I. Hecht is a practicing chiropractor in New York. He is also an adjunct professor at Farmingdale State College and Nassau Community College and an adjunct associate professor at the C.W. Post campus of Long Island University. He teaches courses in medical microbiology, anatomy and physiology, comparative anatomy, human physiology, embryology, and general biology. In addition, he is the course coordinator for Human Biology at Hofstra University where he is an adjunct assistant professor.

Dr. Hecht received his B.S. in Biology–Pre-Medical Studies from Fairleigh Dickinson University in Teaneck, New Jersey. He received his M.S. in Basic Medical Sciences from New York University School of Medicine. He also received his Doctor of Chiropractic (D.C.) degree from New York Chiropractic College in Brookville, New York.

About the Consulting Editor

Consulting editor **David J. Triggle, Ph.D.,** is a SUNY Distinguished Professor and the University Professor at the State University of New York at Buffalo. These are the two highest academic ranks of the university. Professor Triggle received his education in the United Kingdom with a Ph.D. degree in chemistry at the University of Hull. Following post-doctoral fellowships at the University of Ottawa (Canada) and the University of London (United Kingdom) he assumed a position in the School of Pharmacy at the University at Buffalo. He served as chairman of the Department of Biochemical Pharmacology from 1971 to 1985 and as Dean of the School of Pharmacy from 1985 to 1995. From 1996 to 2001 he served as Dean of the Graduate School and from 1999 to 2001 was also the University Provost. He is currently the University Professor, in which capacity he teaches bioethics and science policy, and is President of the Center for Inquiry Institute, a think tank located in Amherst, New York and devoted to issues around the public understanding of science. In the latter respect he is a major contributor to the online M.Ed. program—"Science and The Public"—in the Graduate School of Education and The Center for Inquiry.